OBADIAH

First published July 2016
ISBN: 978-0-9893098-9-9
Visit us on the web!
www.mindijofurby.com
Published by: KingsWynd

KingsWynd exists to fight biblical illiteracy in the church and world. Our goal is to help others love God and become more like Jesus through His Word. We accomplish this through publishing books, articles, curriculum, and Bible studies used by individuals and churches throughout the world.

For more information about KingsWynd, visit www.kingswynd.com

Printed in the United States of America

Scripture, unless otherwise noted, taken from the NEW AMERICAN STANDARD BIBLE®, Copyright © 1960, 1962, 1963, 1968, 1971, 1972, 1973, 1975, 1977, 1995 by The Lockman Foundation. Used by permission.

Author: Mindi Jo Furby
Edited by: Christina Miller
Formatted by: Polgarus Studio

Contents

MAKE Bible Studies

The goal of every Christian is to glorify God and become more like Jesus. The process of realizing this goal is discipleship. Christ chose twelve disciples during His years of ministry on earth and commissioned them to continue the process of making disciples—of helping people become more like Him.

Since I am a disciple of Christ, my prayer is to do the same.

Some try to squeeze the process of discipleship into a concise checklist: "read your Bible," "attend church regularly," etc. We encourage such spiritual disciplines, but by themselves, they don't make disciples. We may gain knowledge, but the end product will mirror the Pharisees more than Jesus.

If we intend to become more like Jesus and help others do the same, we must do as He did. Jesus' method for discipleship was quite simple. *He used relationships fueled by God's Word to produce disciples.*

Jesus didn't instruct His disciples to check off behavioral boxes as they went about their lives. He didn't assign homework involving endless questions and intense reading for them to complete before their next meeting. He lived with them—pouring into their lives and using their relationships (with Himself and each other) as the conduit for spiritual growth and maturity.

If that's how He produced disciples, that's how we should too.

MAKE Bible Studies exist to make disciples by igniting relationships fueled by God's Word. These studies are intensely practical and life-applicable. They're intentionally designed with relationships in mind—first your relationship with God, then your relationships with others in a group setting.

MAKE studies work because they're simple and fiercely poignant. They're designed to be the launching point for discussion, action, and transformation—merging God's truth with life in practical, engaging ways. Be as involved as you want. You have the option of participating in the personal Bible study and commentary as your group moves through the group study or simply showing up for discussion. (Homework is not necessary, though it is helpful.)

The following resources are available for your convenience: an introduction to Obadiah, personal Bible study questions, and passage commentaries for each week. A special note to group leaders: read through the commentary and study guides prior to your group meeting. Pray over the material, make notes, and think of ways to instigate further discussion. Each week, before you begin your study, discuss how your group members incorporated the prior week's challenges into their lives and faith. A leader's guide for the group studies is available at www.kingswynd.com.

Enjoy the journey of becoming more like Jesus through this study of Obadiah. Keep your eyes open and your heart hungry for His transforming power in your life and the lives of your group!

Introduction

"What in the world?"

"I have no clue what's going on."

"Why are we studying this?"

"How are we going to study this for six weeks?"

These are just some of the responses I received the first night of my Obadiah study. Not that I blame them. I knew very little about Obadiah before I chose it as the second MAKE series book. Yet, that's precisely the reason I chose it and why I love studying the lesser-known books of the Bible. It's easy to find multiple studies for "popular" books like John and Romans—they're fantastic and incredibly rich! But books like Obadiah? Books tucked away within the mysterious prophetic books in the latter part of the Old Testament? Those books are scary and intense. And frankly, they're a little depressing with all that war, doom, and gloom.

Lesser-explored territory cries for discovery, and that's what gets my heart pumping. I love showcasing God's creativity and majesty through every book of the Bible, and what better way to do that than by uncovering some hidden gems within the unmined pages?

Obadiah is an intense prophecy spoken by a man we know little about. We tend to find more questions than answers within its pages, but that's what makes a good study: curiosity. Questions fuel interest, interest fuels effort, and effort produces amazing results when the Holy Spirit leads the quest.

So grab a yummy cup of joe and join me on an alluring journey through the tiny book of Obadiah. My prayer is that we'll all have our eyes opened and our hearts transformed by what God has to say.

Week One:
The Weight of Words

OBADIAH 1:1A
PERSONAL BIBLE STUDY QUESTIONS

1. Whose vision is it?

    • What, if anything, do you know about him?

2. Who did the vision come from?

    • Why do you think that is significant?

3. Who/what is the vision about?

    • What, if anything, do you know about him/it?

COMMENTARY

> The vision of Obadiah. Thus says the Lord God concerning
> Edom…
> (Obadiah 1:1a)

***

The first verse of Obadiah is short yet powerful. In it, we learn several crucial things about the book: its author, topic, and original audience. We can discover all this and more within these first words, if we take the time to look.

"THE VISION"

Obadiah begins his book by stating that it is a vision: an account of something he saw and is now describing. The Old Testament contains quite a few visions. In fact, visions and dreams were two of the most common ways God communicated with people in those days. At the time, the Bible as we know it was still being written and put together, so people didn't have the luxury of referring to it whenever they wanted to hear from God. In order to get counsel from God, they either had to visit the tabernacle or temple and perform specific rituals or trust the judgment of the priests and elders.

But sometimes God spoke to people who hadn't sought Him. Consider Noah, who was righteous amidst a perverse generation and who gained God's favor. God spoke to him and told him to build an ark so he, his family, and select animals could survive a global flood (Genesis 6:7-22). We're not told how God spoke to him, only that He did and Noah obeyed.

Abraham has a similar story. He was going about his life as an average man until the day God spoke to him in a vision. God told Abraham to leave his family, country, and life as he knew it, so God could use him to create a nation of people who would bless the earth (Genesis 12:1-3). To our knowledge, Abraham hadn't sought God or desired to be used by Him. But God had other plans, and He used a vision to set in motion one of the greatest stories the earth has ever known.

God used visions to capture people's attention and instruct them to do His will. The word "vision" in Old Testament Hebrew is *chazown* and has a straightforward meaning: "vision (in ecstatic state), vision (in night), vision, oracle, prophecy (divine communication), vision (as title of book of prophecy)."[I] It is used thirty-five times in the Old Testament and is translated as "vision" every single time, which is rare since most Hebrew words can be translated multiple ways in English, depending on the context.

But what exactly was a vision? Did the recipient fall into a trance or completely detach from reality while the vision ran its course? Were visions long, short, or somewhere in between? What did the recipients see, feel, and experience when a vision came upon them? Many of these answers remain elusive, since God doesn't elaborate on them much. But we can deduce a couple of things about them from what He does tell us.

First, God used them to reveal truth to the seer in pictorial form.[II] Visions are vivid and specific images that the recipient would subsequently communicate to others. This is interesting because it is consistent with the way we think. Most people think graphically, not textually. If I told you to think about an elephant, an image of an elephant would probably fill your mind. As the old saying goes, a picture is worth a thousand words. We are far more likely to remember images than words. By using visions, God solidifies the truth He communicates in the minds of the recipients.

One of the most profound, graphic visions in the Bible is that of Isaiah, particularly in chapter six. Isaiah recalls:

In the year of King Uzziah's death I saw the Lord sitting on a throne, lofty and exalted, with the train of His robe filling the temple. Seraphim stood above Him, each having six wings: with two he covered his face, and with two he covered his feet, and with two he flew. And one called out to another and said, "Holy, holy, holy, is the Lord of hosts, the whole earth is full of His glory." And the foundations of the thresholds trembled at the voice of him who called out, while the temple was filling with smoke. Then I said, "Woe is me, for I am ruined! Because I am a man of unclean lips, and I live among a people of unclean lips; for my eyes have seen the King, the Lord of hosts." Then one of the seraphim flew to me with a burning coal in his hand, which he had taken from the altar with tongs. He touched my mouth with it and said, "Behold, this has touched your lips; and your iniquity is taken away and your sin is forgiven." Then I heard the voice of the Lord, saying, "Whom shall I send, and who will go for Us?" Then I said, "Here am I. Send me!" (Isaiah 6:1-8)

This vision launched Isaiah into his calling as a prophet; and what a vision it was! The details are intense and captivate us to the point that we can almost see it too. Visions were powerful and striking, and we can be sure the seers never forgot them!

Second, the best we can tell, visions and dreams were similar in nature. In fact, "it is impossible to draw a sharp line of demarcation between dreams and visions."[III] It would seem that recipients of visions were typically awake (Gen. 15:1-6; Num. 24:1-9; 1 Sam. 3:1-15). Conversely, dreams usually came when the recipients were sleeping (Gen 20:3-7; Gen. 28:12; Gen. 37:5-10; 1 Kings 3:5). Other times, however, there seems to be no direct distinction between the two (Num. 12:6; 2 Sam. 7:4-17). Thus, while there seems to be a slight distinction between the circumstances of dreams and visions, the line between them remains blurred.

Third, "biblical visions concerned both immediate situations…and more distant ones connected with the development of the kingdom of God."[IV] In other words, visions are prophecies. Some focus on the near future while others concern the distant future as far as the end times. One example of an immediate situation is that of Nineveh. In Jonah 1:2, God told Jonah to "'arise, go to Nineveh the great city and cry against it, for their wickedness has come up before Me.'" The citizens of Nineveh were sinning against God at that moment, and He (in His grace) took action to warn them to change their ways. The familiar story traces Jonah's disobedience, but when God brings him back and he finally complies, the people of Nineveh "… believed in God; and they called a fast and put on sackcloth from the greatest to the least of them" (Jonah 3:5). The people of Nineveh listened to God and were spared His impending judgment.

An example of a vision concerning distant times would be when God told Abraham that he would be the father of descendants as numerous as the stars in the sky (Gen. 15:5). Abraham didn't live long enough to see that happen, but he believed God, and God credited it to him as righteousness (Gen 15:6). The scope of visions ranged greatly in both location and time, but every one that originated from God came true (or will come true), exactly as He revealed.

"With perhaps only one exception (Num. 24:4), [visions] were given only to holy men in the service of God, and those of a revelatory nature were always recognized as coming from God."[V] When God appeared to people in visions, the result was the advancement of His glory in some way. Every recipient knew without question that the source of their vision was God. This is crucial because, if Obadiah's vision originated with God, it bears far more weight than if it came from Obadiah (or any other man). Additionally, those who received instruction through the vision would be more highly motivated to obey, since they would have to deal with God if they disobeyed.

Visions occurred frequently in the Old Testament, and the seers were quick to credit them to God. If the seer authored a book of the Bible, the book's introduction would clarify that the vision came from God. (Isaiah 1:1; Ezekiel 1:1; Amos 1:1; Obadiah 1:1; Nahum 1:1; Habakkuk 1:1). Obadiah fits this mold. "The Vision of Obadiah" is actually the "shortest [title] of any Old Testament prophetic book," which is fitting since Obadiah is the shortest book in the Old Testament.[VI] Obadiah wastes no time declaring that his vision is from the Lord and thus should be taken seriously.

When telling people their visions, prophets (including Obadiah) spoke only what God spoke to them. In fact, if they claimed something was from God when it wasn't, they were to be put to death (Deuteronomy 18:20). Visions, dreams, and prophetic words were only as valuable as the Author behind them. The seers and hearers of visions knew they were only the messengers, not the Author of the message.

Here's another way to think of it: an electrical outlet is only as good as its source of electricity. If it isn't attached to a power grid, an outlet is just another piece of plastic and metal. Prophets who weren't "plugged in" to God had nothing of importance to contribute to His message. Those who were plugged in, like Obadiah, spoke with great authority, because they knew the power of their words came from God, not from themselves.

"OF OBADIAH"

Visions came from God and were a vital source of communication between Him and people. While the messengers (usually prophets) who received these visions are important, their identity isn't vital, since they didn't impact the message personally. They simply communicated it.

This is good news for us because Obadiah is perhaps the most elusive prophet in the Old Testament. We are told almost nothing about him.

We don't even know if Obadiah was his proper name, since it means "servant/slave of Yahweh" in Hebrew and could've easily been a title (like we refer to ourselves as disciples of Jesus, Christians, etc.). Malachi is the only other prophet who remains vague like Obadiah, without any identifying information or contextual framework to clue us into his identity.[VII]

Also working against us in identifying Obadiah is the fact that the name was "a common Israelite name in the Old Testament."[VIII] Without clues about his parents, the time when he lived, or the place where he wrote his book, we're left speculating who this messenger of God was. But while we may not have access to as much information as we'd like, we do know more than we initially think.

First, it's probably safe to assume that Obadiah is his proper name.[IX] Again, Obadiah was a common name back then, as the name John is today. Thousands of people have the name John. According to Babycenter.com, it has been within the top fifty names given to boys in the United States within the last five years.[X] So while it is entirely possible that the author simply adapted the name Obadiah because of its meaning, it's likely that it was his proper name.

Second, we know Obadiah was a prophet. Scholar David W. Baker notes that "a special revelation of God has come to Obadiah as it had to others before…an indication that he is included among the prophets."[XI] God chose Obadiah to deliver a message on His behalf, which makes Obadiah one of His ordained prophets, even if he was used only once. (Obadiah may have had other visions, but Scripture records only this one). His message was included in the Canon of Scripture, and that verifies that his vision was, in fact, from God.

Finally, Obadiah (whoever he was) was a man faithful to God. He obeyed God by sharing his vision; otherwise, we wouldn't have the book! This subtle tribute to his faithfulness is quite a big deal. Being a prophet in that day wasn't fun. Most people weren't living for God. Israel had a hard enough time being faithful to Him, let alone other peoples and nations of the world. Because of this, most prophecies involved a promise of judgment if the people didn't turn back to God and a promise of hope if they did. But since people don't like being told what to do (this isn't a new phenomenon in our day and age), when the prophets spoke, people typically didn't receive their words with joy and gladness of heart. Prophets weren't popular, so when they did speak on God's behalf, they were usually taking a huge personal risk of rejection (or worse). Obadiah faithfully spoke the vision God gave him, despite any personal risk involved.

While we don't know much, we know enough about Obadiah to conclude that he was used by God to faithfully deliver a message on His behalf. He was a man available to be used by God and to obey Him when He called—attributes that speak far louder about his character than any biographical details would.

"THUS SAYS THE LORD GOD"

As we discussed, prophets had no doubt where their visions, dreams, and prophecies came from. We might not know the exact process through which God communicated, but we are certain that when He spoke, He made His identity obvious.

Obadiah was no exception. He knew God was the originator of the vision and made it abundantly clear at the beginning of his book by declaring, "Thus says the Lord God" (Oba. 1:1). The proper noun "Lord God" more literally reads "my lord [adonay; title], Yahweh [proper name]."[XII] This is a difficult phrase to translate, but the significance is found not in the title itself but in its placement within the book introduction. This title "indicates the subservient position of the speaker in relation to the addressee, acknowledging the authority of the latter."[XIII] In other words, Obadiah is making it clear that he is speaking God's words, not his own.

While our methods may vary, this isn't a difficult situation to relate to today. We often encounter situations in which we speak on someone else's authority or perhaps allow someone else to speak on our authority. For instance, a doctor may not have the time to respond to every patient's phone call, so he authorizes nurses to respond on his behalf. Or perhaps a student gets in trouble, and his teacher warns him that a repeated infraction will result in suspension. The teacher may not have the sole authority to suspend the student, but because of her familiarity with the school's policies and her solid collegiate relationship with the principal, she can speak in confidence, knowing she'll have the full support of his office.

By using God's name, Obadiah declares that "the source of the message is Yahweh, Israel's covenant God, who is *Lord* and sovereign over all nations and keeper of promises."[XIV] This declaration would also alert his hearers to the potency of the words to come. The "original hearers of the prophecies would [already] expect 'vision' in such a title to mean a message from God through his named prophet."[XV] Obadiah's introduction eradicates any doubt in their minds as well as ours. Obadiah wants his hearers to know he is only the messenger, and that the power of the message comes from its Author, not the human speaker.

"Concerning Edom"

Having firmly established that the vision came from God through His messenger, Obadiah, we move on to the subject of the vision. In this book, the subject is Edom, the descendants of Esau. The prophecy is unique in this regard, for most of the dozen prophetic books in the Old Testament are written directly to Israel, not another nation. Other nations are certainly mentioned and discussed within the parameters of the visions, but most are written by and for Israel.

Obadiah's vision, however, "is directed *to* Edom rather than just being *about* Edom."[XVI] Israel undoubtedly heard the vision (it is in their Old Testament, after all), as word travelled quickly in that day. But Edom is the intended target of this book. A non-Israelite audience links Obadiah with the prophet Jonah, who was also called to deliver a message to non-Israelite people (the Ninevites). We learn far more about Jonah than we ever do Obadiah, but both men would've experienced an extra flare of adversity, having to deliver a message of judgment to people outside their Israelite family.

That said, Edom is closer to Israel (or should be) than the people of Nineveh or any other nation at the time because they are distant relatives. The Edomites came from Esau, Jacob's twin brother and the son of Isaac. The story of Jacob and Esau begins in Genesis 25:21-27:

> Isaac prayed to the Lord on behalf of his wife, because she was barren; and the Lord answered him and Rebekah his wife conceived. But the children struggled together within her; and she said, "If it is so, why then am I this way?" So she went to inquire of the Lord. The Lord said to her, "Two nations are in your womb; and two peoples will be separated from your body; and one people shall be stronger than the other; and the older shall serve the younger." When her days to be delivered were fulfilled, behold, there were twins in her womb. Now the first came forth red, all over like a hairy garment; and they named him Esau. Afterward his brother came forth with his hand holding on to Esau's heel, so his name was called Jacob; and Isaac was sixty years old when she gave birth to them…Esau became a skillful hunter, a man of the field, but Jacob was a peaceful man, living in tents.

Family feuds may start early in life, but not many begin in the womb! Jacob and Esau were bent on conflict before they made their debut into the world. They fought so fiercely that Rebekah worried about the pregnancy. She sought God about it, wanting to know what was going on. Being pregnant with your first is hard enough, with anxiety and worries amidst the excitement of the new adventure. I can't imagine what it was like for Rebekah to have two hooligans warring in her belly!

The womb conflict foreshadowed the future: Jacob and Esau couldn't have been more different. In high school, I knew twin boys who reminded me of Jacob and Esau. One twin was tall, light-skinned, and had a shock of red hair. The other was shorter, darker-skinned, and had dark hair. I had no idea they were twins (or even related) until I learned they had the same last name. Honestly, I still had a hard time believing it for a long while!

Like my high school friends, Jacob and Esau looked and acted very differently. Exacerbating the differences (and conflict) were their parents, who decided to play favorites. Isaac loved Esau, a "man's man," while Rebekah favored Jacob, a "mamma's boy." It's not surprising that the brothers didn't grow up to respect and live harmoniously with one another.

Another glaring difference between them was their worldviews/perspectives. Jacob was a cunning long-term thinker; Esau reacted impulsively and in accordance with whatever made him happy at the moment. For example, one day, Esau came home famished from working in the field. He found Jacob preparing stew and asked for some. Seeing an opportunity, Jacob told Esau that he'd give him stew in exchange for his birthright. In other words, he wanted to trade a quick meal for the blessing and inheritance that was reserved for the firstborn son. While you and I notice the irrationality of that proposal, it was lost on Esau, who declared, "'Behold, I am about to die; so of what use then is the birthright to me?'" (Gen. 25:32). Rash and impulsive much, Esau?

Or was he just "hangry" (severe anger caused by hunger)? Sure enough, Esau swore over his birthright to Jacob in exchange for some lentil stew.

Not surprisingly, this little exchange proved detrimental to their already-fragile relationship. With the help of his mother, Jacob would go on to steal the birthright from Esau by tricking Isaac (since Dad most certainly would not uphold the validity of the stew bargain). Unknowingly, Isaac bestowed the birthright, blessing, and authority upon Jacob—making him master over Esau (Gen. 27:37). By the time Esau discovered Jacob's treachery, it was too late. All Isaac could give him was:

> Behold, away from the fertility of the earth shall be your dwelling, and away from the dew of heaven above. By your sword you shall live, and your brother shall serve; but it shall come about when you become restless, that you will break his yoke from your neck. (Gen. 27:39-40)

Not exactly the most satisfying of blessings! From that point on, Esau's disdain for Jacob became an obsession. He made a vow to kill Jacob after their father died. Fortunately, Rebekah heard Esau's plan and sent Jacob away to live with her brother Laban in Haran until Esau's anger died down (Gen. 27:42-43). Conflict, indeed!

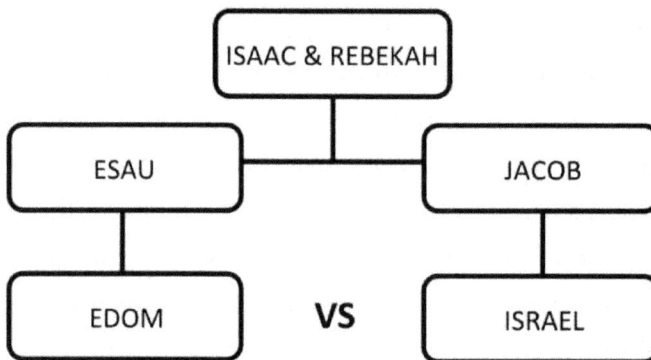

The twins ended up being apart for about twenty years. During that time, both got married (each to more than one woman, which is not advisable) and had several children. As life would have it, they discovered their paths would soon cross again, and Jacob was terrified! All he remembered about his brother was Esau's utter hatred and promise to kill him after their father passed away. To Jacob, seeing Esau meant a run-in with death, so he took every precaution he could think of to avoid that fate.

When they were about to meet, Jacob arranged his family and belongings (along with a sizeable gift) in a specific order, planning to appease Esau with the large gift and hopefully be spared. Turns out, Esau's childish bent toward the temporary overrode his long-term grudge. Instead of charging at Jacob and doing him harm, he "ran to meet him and embraced him, and fell on his neck and kissed him, and they wept" (Gen. 33:4). Quite the happy reunion, though it was short-lived. They parted ways—Esau traveled to Seir and established himself there; Jacob moved on to Shechem in Canaan, where his family would begin their long journey into the Promised Land.

From then on, Esau and Jacob's families (and descendants) had very little interaction. Esau had three wives and several sons. They started the nation of Edom, settling into the Mt. Seir region after destroying the Horites who resided there (Deut. 2:12). Mt. Seir was located in the "mountain and plateau area between the Dead Sea and the Gulf of Aqabah about 100 miles long and up to 40 miles wide."[XVII] It was a convenient location (see map), but the land wasn't fertile, thus fulfilling Isaac's blessing/prophecy over Esau when he said, "… Away from the fertility of the earth shall be your dwelling, and away from the dew of heaven from above" (Gen. 27:39).

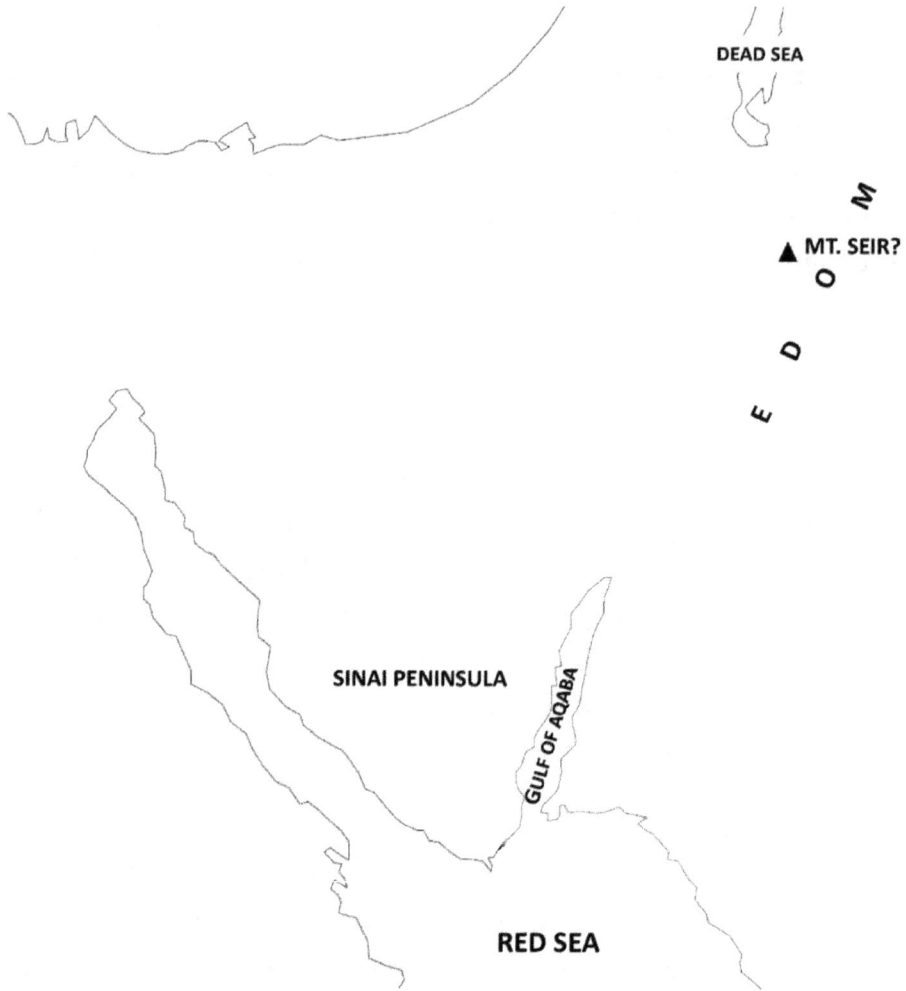

Jacob had four wives, each of whom had sons, which helped grow the tiny nation of Israel. They spent several hundred years in Egypt, first as guests, then as slaves, before the great exodus and wilderness wanderings.

The two nations settled into their respective rhythms of life and didn't cross paths again until hundreds of years after Jacob's death. When they did, they quickly realized that any peace between them had fizzled with the passing years.

When the Israelites left Egypt, they circled Mt. Seir for many days (Deut. 2:1). God then told them via Moses,

> "You have circled this mountain long enough. Now turn north, and command the people, saying, 'You will pass through the territory of your brothers the sons of Esau who live in Seir; and they will be afraid of you. So be very careful; do not provoke them, for I will not give you any of their land, even as little as a footstep because I have given Mount Seir to Esau as a possession. You shall buy food from them with money so that you may eat, and you shall also purchase water from them with money so that you may drink.'" (Deut. 2:3-6)

God wanted them to move forward, and the best way to do so was to travel through the land of Edom (a.k.a. Seir). Moses obeyed God and sent messengers to the king of Edom, requesting permission to pass through their land. He assured him that the people of Israel wouldn't deviate to the right or to the left, nor would they take anything to eat or drink. Seems pretty reasonable, but the king of Edom didn't think so. He replied, "You shall not pass through us, or I will come out with the sword against you" (Num. 20:18b). This reply fulfills Isaac's prophecy over Esau once again, for he said, "By your sword you shall live" (Gen. 27:40a).

Moses tried yet again to gain the king's permission, but to no avail. He was once again rejected:

> But he said, "You shall not pass through." And Edom came out against him with a heavy force and with a strong hand. Thus Edom refused to allow Israel to pass through his territory; so Israel turned away from him. (Num. 20:20-21)

Israel and Edom were no longer on friendly terms, and it would only get worse. The rest of their history together would be marked by war and bloodshed. When Saul became king several generations later, he fought against Edom and punished them, though was never able to fully conquer them (1 Sam. 14:47). David then became king and overcame Edom completely and made them servants, fulfilling Isaac's prophecy yet again—"... your brother you shall serve ..." (2 Sam. 8:14; Gen. 27:40). Solomon continued the reign over Edom when he became king. As an adversary, he maintained control and "made the Edomite cities Ezion Geber and Eloth, on the Gulf of Aqabah, seaports from which his ships sailed to Ophir."[XVIII]

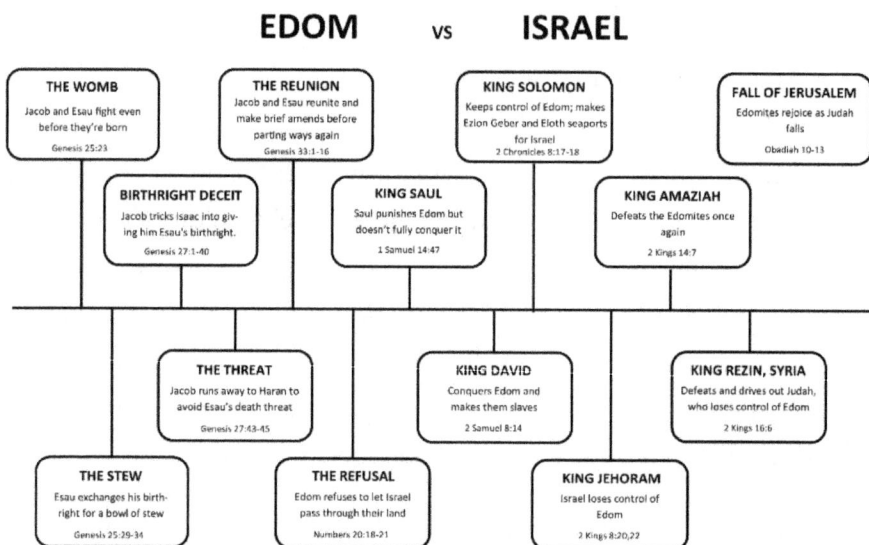

EDOM vs ISRAEL

THE WOMB	THE REUNION	KING SOLOMON	FALL OF JERUSALEM
Jacob and Esau fight even before they're born	Jacob and Esau reunite and make brief amends before parting ways again	Keeps control of Edom; makes Ezion Geber and Eloth seaports for Israel	Edomites rejoice as Judah falls
Genesis 25:23	Genesis 33:1-16	2 Chronicles 8:17-18	Obadiah 10-13

BIRTHRIGHT DECEIT	KING SAUL	KING AMAZIAH
Jacob tricks Isaac into giving him Esau's birthright.	Saul punishes Edom but doesn't fully conquer it	Defeats the Edomites once again
Genesis 27:1-40	1 Samuel 14:47	2 Kings 14:7

THE THREAT	KING DAVID	KING REZIN, SYRIA
Jacob runs away to Haran to avoid Esau's death threat	Conquers Edom and makes them slaves	Defeats and drives out Judah, who loses control of Edom
Genesis 27:43-45	2 Samuel 8:14	2 Kings 16:6

THE STEW	THE REFUSAL	KING JEHORAM
Esau exchanges his birthright for a bowl of stew	Edom refuses to let Israel pass through their land	Israel loses control of Edom
Genesis 25:29-34	Numbers 20:18-21	2 Kings 8:20,22

When the kingdom of Israel split into Israel (the northern kingdom) and Judah (the southern kingdom), they lost control of Edom. During the reign of Jehoram, Edom revolted against Israel and wiggled her way to freedom around 847 BC (2 Kings 8:20, 22). Around fifty years later, Amaziah (a Judean king), severely defeated the Edomites.[XIX] About sixty years after that, Rezen, king of Syria, warred against Judah and captured

Eloth, the city Solomon made a seaport for Israel. Judeans were driven out, once again losing control of Edom (2 Kings 16:6). The battling continued through the fall of Jerusalem in 586 BC by the Babylonians. This historic event left the Edomites (Esau's descendants) rejoicing over Israel's downfall and taking over the southern part of Palestine.[xx] Confused? Don't be! There's a nifty chart (above) to help you keep it all straight.

The history between Edom and Israel is bitter and wrought with turmoil and hatred. It's not surprising that God has a word for the Edomites, and Obadiah is just the man to deliver it. We will soon work our way into the vision itself. But for now, let's pause and see how these first few words of Obadiah can challenge and spur us on to greater depths of faith. After all, knowledge is limited to mere real estate in our brains unless we exercise it and apply it to our lives.

Anonymity Doesn't Equal Obscurity

As we've seen, God chose the mysterious Obadiah to deliver His Word to Edom. Not knowing much about him is great news, because if God can use him, He can most certainly use us!

We tend to think God uses only extraordinary men and women who have something magnificent to offer. It's easy to get self-conscious about our faith when we hear stories like David and Goliath, Paul's missionary journeys, or modern-day revivalists who've done world-changing work for God. How can God use little ol' me to do anything substantial for His kingdom? How could my relatively boring life possibly make a difference for eternity?

Obadiah shows us that anonymity to the world doesn't mean anonymity to God. In fact, it often means just the opposite—being known, prized, and prominent. Obadiah wasn't popular as a man, nor is the book he wrote. Let's be honest, it's the shortest book in the Old Testament, often overlooked by just about everyone. Despite all these challenges, God Himself has preserved Obadiah's voice and vision for thousands of years, keeping them alive for us to read today. Not so anonymous to Him!

While we will not receive that kind of lasting recognition by serving God (the Bible is complete, after all), He can still use us to make a huge difference in this world. He knows, loves, and cherishes each of us personally (2 Thessalonians 2:16). We are not obscure! This means that as long as we're still breathing, God can, does, and wants to use us in mighty ways for His glory. All we have to do is follow Obadiah's footsteps: be available, be obedient, and exercise our faith in God through Jesus Christ. God will take care of the rest, and I think Obadiah would agree that it's always worth it! Following God may not be easy (Obadiah's vision wasn't exactly pleasant news to deliver), but when we do, He transforms the mediocre into the magnificent, the undistinguished into the unimaginable.

Obedience Travels

We, like Obadiah, may never know the reach of our obedience. I highly doubt Obadiah knew that his vision would transcend all of time and reach the homes of billions of people all over the world. He probably thought it would reach one small nation, maybe two, then disappear into the abyss. But God had a different idea.

A modern-day example of God using the ordinary for something extraordinary is found in the story of a man named Nate, born in 1923 as the seventh of eight children near Philadelphia, Pennsylvania. He seemed to live a mediocre life in an average family. He wasn't a child prodigy, nor did he have remarkable skills that set him apart in any special way. At the ripe age of thirteen, Nate accepted Christ as his Savior and often prayed for God to show him the right way. Thousands of teenagers do the same every day in youth groups across the nation. That's fantastic—and we rejoice right alongside the angels in heaven—but it's nothing superbly out of the ordinary.

At age eighteen, Nate discovered his passion—aviation—and spent the next several years involving himself in different aviation venues. He got married at twenty-five and decided to combine his aviation skills with his newfound passion for missions work, and he and his wife set out for Ecuador to help establish a mission airbase. This decision reveals Nate's commitment to following God's leading. Like Obadiah, he responded when God called, and he and his bride headed off to a foreign land.

It seemed God was answering his prayer for guidance as he and his wife settled into Ecuadorian life. In addition to setting up the base, Nate and his team began reaching out to different Ecuadorian people groups— dropping baskets of supplies from their plane in hopes of beginning a peaceful relationship so they could eventually share the gospel with them. They had success until one day in early January, 1956, when sudden tragedy struck. Nate and his team landed on the beach, where they had been reaching out to the Auca Indians. Instead of furthering peaceful advances, they were brutally martyred.

Not exactly the happy ending we'd expect, right? What good could possibly come from men obeying God and subsequently losing their lives in a tragic (and avoidable) act of murder? As the story unfolds, we see that God had big plans for the families of the martyrs and for the Auca people. Nate's sister, Rachel, ended up living with the Aucas for forty years, leading many to Christ. Nate's son, Steve, followed in his father's footsteps by becoming a pilot and joining the service to the Aucas. Not only did many of the Indian tribe come to accept Christ, but Steve also befriended one of his father's murders, a man named Mincaye, who also accepted Jesus Christ as his Savior. I have had the privilege of hearing Steve and Mincaye speak together in person, and my skin still breaks out in goosebumps as I recall them together on that stage.

It's amazing to see what God can do from the simplest acts of obedience. Like Obadiah, Nate obeyed God's promptings and guidance. Things didn't turn out as he or his family planned, but God's sovereignty extended far beyond their miniscule imaginations and ended up bringing an entire village to saving knowledge of Him. We will see hundreds of people in heaven one day because of their obedience. There's no better result than that.

Obedience to God requires sacrifice and accepting a lot of unknowns. But the unknown and unseen are part of the thrill of obeying God like Obadiah and Nate did. God will take our obedience to heights we never imagined, and we won't know its full reach until we get to heaven.

Words are Weighty

Obeying God in the anonymity of life yields big results, and one truth Obadiah realized amidst his obedience is that words are weighty. Obadiah's words were powerful because they were not his own. When he spoke, he spoke on God's behalf, faithfully delivering His message whether people wanted to hear it or not.

The challenge for us is to do the same. We may not receive a divine vision and receive a calling to deliver it to an obstinate people. But God has given us a message, and it's the best news this world has ever received: the gospel. In 2 Corinthians 5:17-20, God tells us:

> Therefore if anyone is in Christ, he is a new creature; the old things passed away; behold, new things have come. Now all these things are from God, who reconciled us to Himself through Christ and gave us the ministry of reconciliation, namely, that

God was in Christ reconciling the world to Himself, not counting their trespasses against them, and He has committed to us the word of reconciliation. Therefore, we are ambassadors for Christ, as though God were making an appeal through us; we beg you on behalf of Christ, be reconciled to God.

When we accept Christ as Savior, we are made His ambassadors to the world. Just as a US ambassador represents the Unites States in whatever country he's stationed in, so we represent Jesus to this world, which is our temporary home. As Christians, we receive a new identity and a new purpose in life: to be God's hands, feet, heart, and voice to this world.

Because of our status as ambassadors, our words matter. If we bear the name Christian, people look at us with higher expectations (or at least, they should). We tend to think our words don't make that much of a difference, but that couldn't be further from the truth. Our words matter because of Who they represent, and like Obadiah, we should do our best to get out of the way and let God speak through us to people in our lives.

In the Scripture, God says a lot about our words. He mentions the tongue over one hundred times, teaching us (among many things) that our tongues are tools and can be used for good or evil. Our task is to submit our words to God. James even goes so far as to say that

> If anyone thinks himself to be religious, and yet does not bridle his tongue but deceives his own heart, this man's religion is worthless. So also the tongue is a small part of the body, and yet it boasts of great things. See how great a forest is set aflame by such a small fire! (James 1:26; 3:5)

A tiny part of our body boasts a whole lot of power. Obadiah recognized this and humbled himself to speak with caution as God directed him. We must do the same. Our words bear weight because we bear the name of God. People are watching us, and we have the power to influence their perception of God by what we say and how we act. Talk about pressure! We can do some serious damage, misrepresenting Him, if we let our tongues run loose. Just the same, we can bring healing, hope, and joy to people by using words that glorify Him and edify others. God is sovereign and gracious, forgiving us when we err; but how much easier (and better) will life be if we exercise a bit more caution with our words?

God gives us opportunities every day to build others up, and we accomplish that largely by what we say. How have your words been lately? Do they draw people closer to God or shove them further away from Him?

***

Obadiah was an anonymous man whose obedience to God and caution with words unleashed God's power and kingdom here on earth. God desires to use us powerfully for His glory as well. Will you let Him take the reins in your life this week? Will you obey Him and use your words with caution, recognizing that you represent Him in all you do and say? Let's learn from Obadiah and allow God to use us as His great ambassadors!

GROUP STUDY

INTRO

> Death and life are the in power of the tongue, and those who love
> it will eat its fruit. (Proverbs 18:21)

Our mouths are powerful tools that can be used both for good and for evil.
We all have regretted words we've spoken in haste or out of anger, and we
all have been hurt by the words of others.

1. Share a time when you said something you shouldn't have and
   immediately regretted it (or when someone hurt you in the same
   way).

2. Now share a time when you were encouraged/lifted up by
   someone's words. How did those words impact you?

THE WORD

The tiny book of Obadiah tells us a lot about the power of words. In the
first verse, we sense their heavy weight:

The vision of Obadiah. Thus says the Lord God concerning Edom…

But first things first.

1. Whose vision is it?

   • What do you know about him?
   • What do you know about visions in the Bible, especially
     in the prophetic books?

2. Who/what is the vision about?

   • What do you know about him/it?

3. Where did the vision come from?

   • Why do you think that's significant?
   • Read Deuteronomy 18:20. Would you want to be in the position of a prophet of God? Why or why not?

APPLY

While the specific office (not gift) of the prophet ceased with the conclusion of the canon, we have a lot more in common with prophets than we realize, namely that our words bear some serious God-weight.

1. According to 2 Corinthians 5:17-20, what ministry have we (as Christians) been given?

   • What position/office does that put us in when it comes to the world (v. 20a)?
   • Whom do we represent when we speak? Why is that significant?

2. James tells us, "The tongue is a small part of the body, and yet it boasts of great things. See how great a forest is set aflame by such a small fire!" (James 3:5). And also, "If anyone thinks himself to be religious, and yet does not bridle his tongue but deceives his own heart, this man's religion is worthless" (James 1:26).

- How have you been using your tongue lately? Do your "tongue fires" glorify God and consume people with His glory, or do they destroy others and hinder the expansion of His kingdom on earth?
- What can you do this week to let God reign over your tongue and use your words to draw others closer to Him instead of driving them further away?

PRAY

Share prayer requests and encourage one another to apply the truths learned this week.

WEEK TWO:
THE PUFF OF PRIDE

OBADIAH 1:1B-4
PERSONAL BIBLE STUDY QUESTIONS

1. Who is the report from (1:1)?

2. Where has the envoy been sent (1:1)?

3. Speaking against Edom, what does God say has deceived them (1:3)?

   - Have you ever deceived yourself in this way? Describe a time when you thought a bit too highly of yourself only to be knocked down with a good dose of humility.

4. What did the Edomites say in their hearts that revealed their pride (1:3)?

   - Think of a time when you thought you were getting away with something you shouldn't have been doing—gossip, dishonesty, an affair, disobedience, etc. What happened?

How long did it last before you were found out (if you were)? What happened when the truth came out?

5. Is any place too high or far for God to reach and take control (1:4)?

COMMENTARY

> We have heard a report from the Lord, and an envoy has been sent among the nations saying, "Arise and let us go against her for battle"—"Behold, I will make you small among the nations; you are greatly despised. The arrogance of your heart has deceived you, you who live in the clefts of the rock, in the loftiness of your dwelling place, who say in your heart, 'Who will bring me down to earth?' Though you build high like the eagle, though you set your nest among the stars, from there I will bring you down," declares the Lord. (Obadiah 1b-4)

***

Have you ever been in a situation that desperately calls for truth, yet no one speaks up? You may be in a room full of smart people who are having a dumb moment, yet you're scared to say anything. Or perhaps a friend is making gross mistakes parenting, and you're not sure it's your place to interfere. Or maybe current events or politics get your blood pumping. What would you give to be able to pop into a congressional meeting and speak your mind freely?

If you're like me, you've daydreamed of (and possibly acted out within the privacy of your home) what you would say in these kinds of situations if you didn't have to worry about political correctness and unpleasant ramifications. I wouldn't mind securing a captive audience with a couple of choice people in my life—or some government officials, for that matter! Of course, I realize that everything I say is only my opinion, and everyone is entitled to one of those. But still...

Obadiah had the opportunity of a lifetime with his vision. He not only got to confront a bunch of ruffians (the Edomites) about their sin, but he also got to do so under the sovereign authority of God Himself! And he knew he was saying the perfect thing at the perfect time! He didn't have to rehash his words later, wishing he had spoken differently. God's words were so powerfully manifested through him, Obadiah got to speak with the boldness of a lion charging into a pack of gazelles. He may have been nervous at first, but I bet once he got going, he was on fire with the message God breathed into his lungs.

By this point in our study, Obadiah has made it clear that his vision is straight from God. He was chosen as the messenger and obediently submitted to the task, but that's all he says about the vision. Every word from here until nearly the end of the prophecy is the vision from God.

"WE HAVE HEARD A REPORT FROM THE LORD"

When we study the Bible, especially trickier passages like those found in the Minor Prophets, it is wise go slow, ask questions, and clarify even the smallest details. For instance, the beginning of Obadiah's vision is a report from the Lord that "we" have heard. Most of the time you and I would move right past that detail onto something that catches our attention more vividly. But when we do that, we miss out on foundational cornerstones that help establish the vision more securely in our minds.

The "we" Obadiah refers to here is most likely himself and Israel.[XXI] Again, Obadiah is most likely an Israelite, identifying with God's people.[XXII] Even though his vision is addressed to and about Edom, Israel would've received the vision too because it originated with their God. The faithful prized words from the Lord back then just as they do now, so it's not surprising that Israel is included in the vision as witnesses to God's hand at work.

Now that we know who "we" is, let's look at the "report" they heard from the Lord. Nothing inherently special is discovered from a word study of "report." In Hebrew, the word is *shemuw'ah*, which means "report, news, rumour, tidings, mention."[XXIII]

While the word itself may not be all that interesting, its author certainly is! Just as Obadiah's vision is from the Lord, so is this report. God is cuing Israel into something He's doing with Edom, which would have made headlines if they'd had newspapers back then.

Wouldn't it be awesome if God gave you a report of how He was working in your life, particularly if it involved one of your enemies? While our definition of "enemy" is diluted because of our cushy culture, we still undoubtedly have people in our lives who would qualify.

Let's say a superior at work decides (for whatever reason) that he doesn't like you, and his number-one mission in life is to make you miserable. You pray about it every day, hold your tongue, and do whatever you can to keep the peace. You fully expect things to get better, but they don't. You're doing everything right and he's still a pill. Some days it escalates to the point that you call in sick because you just can't deal with it. Then God does something miraculous. Through your devotions one morning, He speaks to you—audibly. He tells you everything is going to be all right and that your superior won't be an issue for you much longer. What a dandy "report"! Now going to work is no longer a drag. Far from it! You're excited to go, if only to see how God is going to deal with your ever-annoying superior.

Has your situation changed by just hearing the report? No. Your superior is still there and still treats you like scum in the backwoods swamps of the South. But your attitude is different because hope has been infused into the deepest part of your soul. You have it on the highest authority that the boss won't be an issue much longer. You don't know what will happen or how, but knowing that God's moving in that situation is good enough for you. Bring it on, Mr. Boss Man!

That's what's going on for Israel through Obadiah's vision. As we discussed last week, Edom and Israel weren't exactly on friendly terms. Their history was wrought with tension and bloodshed, and Israel wouldn't be the least bit disappointed if God did something to get rid of Edom. Hearing a report—any report—about them would be welcome news, but not even they can imagine just how good the news will be.

"AND AN ENVOY HAS BEEN SENT AMONG THE NATIONS SAYING"

Obadiah's vision begins with Israel (and Obadiah by association) hearing a report from the Lord concerning their enemy Edom. But the report isn't limited to Israel or Edom. Turns out several other nations hear something too.

The word "envoy" used here is unique. It's a rare Hebrew word, *sir*, that is found nowhere else except in biblical poetry (Prov. 13:17; 25:13; Isa. 18:2; 57:9).[XXIV] This word is difficult to distinguish from another Hebrew word for "messenger" or "angel" (*malak*), for it carries such a similar definition and meaning.[XXV] Thus, we should think of it as synonymous with a group of messengers.

We aren't too familiar with the concept of messengers, because we simply don't need them in our culture. Thanks to modern technology and social media, it takes mere seconds to get in touch with someone, no matter where they are in the world. As I write this, my husband is on a business trip in Taiwan, and we just talked face to face via modern-day technology. We're a spoiled culture, for sure! Not so in the ancient world, however. They didn't have luxuries like phones and internet, and their concept of "snail mail" involved camels and days of traveling through sandy deserts. The envoy here refers to a messenger who hand-delivered a pronouncement to a targeted audience on their master's behalf. They delivered these messages orally and/or in writing.[XXVI]

One famous decree that gives us a great glimpse of the messenger's work is found within the Old Testament story of Esther. A man named Haman had his eyes on power, and a Jew named Mordecai stood in his way. Haman tricked the king into issuing a decree against the Jews in retaliation for Mordecai's perceived disrespect:

> Then the king's scribes were summoned on the thirteenth day of the first month, and it was written just as Haman commanded to the king's satraps, to the governors who were over each province and to the princes of each people, each province according to its script, each people according to its language, being written in the name of King Ahasuerus and sealed with the king's signet ring. Letters were sent by couriers to all the king's provinces to destroy, to kill and to annihilate all the Jews, both young and old, women and children, in one day, the thirteenth day of the twelfth month, which is the month Adar, and to seize their possessions as plunder. A copy of the edict to be issued as law in every province was published to all the peoples so that they should be ready for this day. The couriers went out impelled by the king's command while the decree was issued at the citadel in Susa. (Esther 3:12-15a)

Quite the process! Of course, not all envoys and messengers went to such elaborate lengths to communicate their messages, but the formula remains the same. Certain men were chosen by an authority figure to convey a specific message to an intended audience. Messengers were important people, similar to ambassadors, for they spoke their master's words with their master's authority.

Obadiah knows that a message has gone out, and the intended audience is quite large. The recipients of this particular envoy are "the nations," which can mean a lot of things, depending on the context. The Hebrew word for nations is *gowy*, which retains a straightforward meaning of "nations" or "peoples."[XXVII] It is used approximately 560 times in the Hebrew concordance of the NASB, yet here it probably refers to the enemies of Edom (which the message itself will confirm).[XXVIII]

An envoy of messengers has been sent out to Edom's enemies. Israel is probably beyond ready to hear the message, and so are we!

"Arise and Let Us Go Against Her for Battle"

The envoy's message is one of war—the nations are being summoned for battle. The "us" here refers to the nations, Edom's enemies. "Her" is a reference to Edom. Thus, the nations are gathering to go against Edom for battle—definitely not a situation I envy for Edom!

There's no doubt that God is sovereignly involved in this ensuing battle, even if He's not directly commanding it.[XXIX] (Edom's enemies weren't exactly God-fearing folk, so they wouldn't have listened to Him even if He did). One of my favorite aspects of God is His sovereignty—His supreme power and authority over anything and everything in this world. Even when situations seem horrendous, God is in control and works everything out for the good of those who love Him and are called according to His purposes.[XXX]

God's message through Obadiah begins with the gathering of her enemies for battle. Things aren't looking great for Edom, and it's about to get worse.

"Behold, I Will Make You Small Among the Nations; You Are Greatly Despised."

When we want to get someone's attention, we use exclamation points and words like "Look!" When God wants to draw extra emphasis to something in His Word, He uses words like "behold" and "truly." The message is the same: "Pay attention!" Everything God says should hold our attention. It is certainly capturing the focus of the Israelites who are eavesdropping on Obadiah's vision. But God wants us to pay extra attention now, so He uses the literary method of interjection to get us to do so.

The word "behold" in Hebrew is *hinneh*, and it is used well over a thousand times in the Hebrew concordance of the NASB.[XXXI] My initial thought after learning this staggering number is that we must have pretty thick skulls to be told to pay attention that many times! I know it's true for me. I read something over and over again—so many times that I could quote it back to you, yet the truth remains lodged in my head instead of filtering down to flood my heart. We need to pay attention, and with more than a cursory glance. This might not be the sole reason God uses emphatic words, but I'm sure it contributes at least slightly. Our job as readers is to pay attention to textual cues like this one and do what we're told. If God wants us to pay extra attention to something he says, let's obey and give it!

After getting our attention, He tells us that someone will take personal action. That someone ("I") refers to God. He is the one speaking and He's talking to Edom ("you"). The first part of His message isn't pleasant—He promises to make Edom small among the nations. While this is a prophecy about the future, it's also a pretty good description of Edom from the beginning until that point in history. Edom had always been small, never gaining clout or status among the nations. She stood in a decent geographical location, having access to some fertile ground and sources of water, but nothing terribly significant. The Edomite people made their living primarily by mining copper ore and by "controlling the roads that ran from Arabia and the Red Sea to Damascus and to Gaza and the Mediterranean."[XXXII] That helped them survive, but not as a booming economy.

But the smallness spoken of here doesn't refer to real estate. In fact, "size was usually not an issue, since most other regional states in the area, such as Moab, Ammon, Israel, Judah, and the Philistines, were not geographically large."[XXXIII] God is instead referring to their significance, prestige, and honor. Those who were "small" were synonymously "despised," as the second half of this verse specifies.[XXXIV] Edom was small both geographically and in significance, and it was only going to get worse.

As stated, God wants to make sure we (and the Israelites and Edom) understand this point: *Edom will be cut down in significance and honor among the nations, and He will be the One holding the chainsaw.* God is involved in the ensuing battle. He is sovereignly orchestrating Edom's demise, and oh, what a demise it will be!

"The Arrogance of Your Heart Has Deceived You"

We now begin to see the reason behind all the hostility projected onto Edom. Until this point, we almost feel bad for them—as if they're getting picked on just because they're runts. God, of course, has better reasons than that for inflicting punishment on people. At this point, we peek into His long list of charges against them.

The first charge is a doozy—arrogance. We immediately learn two things about this particular charge: one, that Edom struggled with arrogance; and two, that the struggle is so intense, they have lost touch with reality.

Pride is no small sin in God's eyes, as He makes obvious hundreds of times throughout His Word. In Proverbs 8:13, He says, "The fear of the Lord is to hate evil; pride and arrogance and the evil way and the perverted mouth, I hate." Anything that is tantamount to evil and hatred in God's eyes can't be good, and that's exactly what He thinks of pride.

At its core, pride is idolatry. It's placing yourself above God, thereby completely disregarding the two great commandments: "Love the Lord your God with all your heart, and with all your soul, and with all your mind" and "Love your neighbor as yourself" (Matt. 22:37b, 39b). Pride turns the great commandments into "Love myself with all my heart, soul, and mind; love myself more than all others." Our capacity to love others is completely stripped when pride seeps in, because it puts the attention on ourselves. Such an attitude stands in blatant contrast with who God is and who He created us to be.

G.K. Chesterton once said, "If I had only one sermon to preach it would be a sermon against pride." Powerful words from one of the greatest writers, theologians, and speakers of all time! He understood the cancerous nature of pride—how the tiniest molecule can sneak into your soul and ravage it until it's entirely contaminated and separated from God. That's what happened with Edom. They allowed pride into their hearts (unjustifiably, I might add, since they weren't all that great), and went straight downhill from there.

While pride is bad, the side effects it produces are infinitely worse. Edom suffered from a terrible one: self-deceit. Pride inherently comes with an I'm-better-than-you mentality, which quickly leads to self-deception. Chances are, the higher you think of yourself, the lower the rest of the world thinks about you. I've met people who can't hold down a job for more than a couple of years at a time. When asked about it, they blame it solely on their employers not being fair, not recognizing their talents, etc. Reality has gone out the window for these "victims." Sorry, friend, but at some point, it's not them … it is you!

That's one reason pride is so dangerous—it puts us completely at odds with reality. Reality begins with God and His Word. Our world is magnificent, yet marred; beautiful, yet broken; stunning, yet sad. God acknowledges the corruption and is in the process of redeeming us from it. One day we who believe will stand before Him in a new heaven and a new earth, completely restored, made whole, and set free from sin. This is what keeps us going; this is what gives us hope.

But the world would have us think the exact opposite. The world wants us to think we exist for the here and now and should do whatever possible to make ourselves happy. When this is our mindset, it's easy to limit our sights horizontally to one another and let the comparison games begin. If this life is as good as it's going to get, then I might be better than the people around me. If I make more money, have more toys, have fewer wrinkles, am in better shape, and have the most friends, I win. And if that's the case, I have every right to be proud, because I managed to secure everything for myself. God is completely out of the picture, which leaves all the more room for me.

Edom fell into this mindset. They succumbed to a secular worldview instead of God's and allowed their circumstances to dictate their identity. When things went well for them, they became boastful and thought they'd done it themselves. They ignored God entirely, thus deceiving themselves and living in an alternative (and erroneous) reality.

Pride digs its claws into people until it rips them from reality and thrusts them into sin-drenched lunacy. Edom willingly fell prey to this fate, and God isn't finished calling them out on it.

"You Who Live in the Clefts of the Rock, in the Loftiness of Your Dwelling Place"

As with most people, Edom succumbed to pride in their physical circumstances—things that were ultimately out of their control. I find it humorous when we boast about things that can easily be taken away—

money, health, status, etc. With one dip of the stock market, the wealthy can become the needy. With one doctor's appointment, the strong can be declared sickly. With one social blunder, the favored can become the despised. We can manage our circumstances but we can't control them.

One such circumstance (and source of pride) for Edom was a geographical perk where they lived. The "clefts of the rock" and "loftiness of your dwelling place" mentioned in this verse refer to the "rocky impenetrability as well as the height of the Edomite plateau."[XXXV] Edom was located high above the surrounding valleys below, and "the natural cliffs and ravines edging her land provided inaccessible fastness and were ideal for guerrilla activity."[XXXVI]

Their location made it easy for them to control important trade routes. In order to pass through this territory, one would need to travel "through narrow passages between towering rocks, a way that is easily blocked by a few well-placed soldiers."[XXXVII] It's little wonder they grew cocky in their lofty dwellings. Edom believed themselves impenetrable, trusting the fortresses of their geography with no regard to their theology.

It's kind of like the story of two fleas caught in a bitter argument about which one owned the best part of the dog. Edom's location may have been fabulous, but it was still on a decaying earth. A dog is a dog is a dog; a location is a location is a location. Without God, it's all irrelevant, fleeting, and completely insecure—definitely not something to get cocky about.

"Who Say in Your Heart, 'Who Will Bring Me Down to Earth?'"

One problem with living for the world is that we forget the One who created it. Edom mastered the art of looking down on people. What began as a physical posture from a lofty dwelling place soon crept into a spiritual and emotional posture of the heart—puffing themselves up to the point that all else was beneath them, including God.

Our hearts are easily impressionable and misguided. We can be devastated by a single word dumped on us by someone we love; we can also soar with even the slightest bit of good news. And that's just from an emotional standpoint. The spiritual state of our hearts is much more grim, thanks to sin. Jeremiah 17:9 says that "the heart is more deceitful than all else and is desperately sick; who can understand it?" This single verse reveals God's truth about the heart and destroys the cultural propaganda that "following your heart" will grant you happiness.

Edom followed their hearts and it led to unjustified egotism. In the process, they did something we all do—heart speak. We talk to ourselves all the time. Maybe not out loud (psychologists tend to frown at that behavior), but our brains constantly weigh options, make decisions, and confront people in ways we wouldn't dare do face-to-face.

Edom talked to themselves too, and it resulted in arrogance. They told themselves they were the best and soon started believing it. They thought they were impermeable and, sure enough, believed it to be an infallible perspective. They asked, "Who will bring me down to earth?" thinking it an impossible feat for anyone. While that may have been true at some level geographically, they forgot the One who resides far above the earth and is sovereign over every inch of it.

"'THOUGH YOU BUILD HIGH LIKE THE EAGLE, THOUGH YOU SET YOUR NEST AMONG THE STARS"

We understand pride with imagery of height—being "puffed up" or "lofty" describes the haughty person well. Such imagery is fitting, for it shows where we think we live: above everyone else. In this verse, God taps into this imagery and gives us a fantastic word picture describing Edom's pride. He compares it to eagles who build their nests high, so high they appear to be among the stars.

The "eagle" probably references the imperial eagle or griffon vulture, which were indigenous to that particular area.[XXXVIII] Eagles are fascinating creatures, often associated with power and prestige because of their regal appearance and their incredible feats of strength and swiftness as hunters.[XXXIX] God references them several times throughout Scripture, both literally (Deut. 14:12) and figuratively (Deut. 28:49, 32:11; Job 9:26). While they weren't common, they were known and familiar to the people living in that time and region.

Grant me a moment for a brief interlude. Isn't it amazing how God communicates with us in numerous ways through His Word? Not only does He use a myriad of literary devices (like the simile of the eagle used here), but He also uses nature and known life circumstances to illustrate truth. His Word reflects Himself—creative, stimulating, engaging, impactful, and intense. There's nothing monotonous, dull, or boring about Him or His Word. He gives us rich word pictures and lustrous illustrations. Be sure you take time to imagine them as you read them.

Imagine an eagle soaring through a windless day as the sun warms its feathers in mid-flight. Can you see it swooping down to pick choice branches for its nest? Or picture it delivering a freshly snatched meal to chirping eaglets? Scripture is way too important to leave on a page. When you read it, engage with it, because when you do, you engage with its Author. Allow any imagery to take you on a journey guided by the Holy Spirit, who fervently waits to transform your life through it.

Back to the word picture here in Obadiah. Eagles build their nests "in inaccessible places, far from human and animal marauders."[XL] These nests are typically about five feet in diameter (sometimes up to nine feet after multiple annual uses), and can weigh up to two tons.[XLI] Can you imagine such a feat? How fun would it be to watch a magnificent bird build an enormous nest like that? I think a simple sparrow's nest is fascinating. I can hardly imagine being up close and personal to an eagle's aerie.

These nests are what God targets when He compares Edom to eagles. Edom and eagles had something in common: their homes were located well above their surrounding neighbors—high as if "among the stars." This naturally gave way to pride. Edom, like eagles, felt safe in their surroundings as if they couldn't be breached. But unlike the eagle, who has no natural predators, Edom has several. And they're all at the beck and call of the Hound of Heaven.

"'FROM THERE I WILL BRING YOU DOWN,' DECLARES THE LORD."

We mentioned earlier how pride puts us into an alternate reality, separated from God. Pride severs our relationship with Him and leaves us to operate within the confines of the world's perspective, which isn't reality at all. In their pride, Edom thought they were invincible to the point they had completely forgotten about God. But through Obadiah's vision, God is about to regain their attention in a sobering way.

If another nation couldn't bring Edom down, God would, and He promises as much in this verse. Once again, God reveals Himself as the Source behind whatever is about to happen to Edom. We know He will make them "small among the nations," even if we aren't yet sure how.

God's sovereign hand is involved in everything that occurs on this earth—either directly by first-hand action or indirectly by allowance. Job's story reveals that the devil can't do anything without God's permission (Job 1:6-12). God actively restrains evil in this world (2 Thess. 2:7), even when we can't see it (at least in ways that are satisfying to us). In the same breath, He constantly bestows gifts and mercies upon us, even while we live in a decaying world (James 1:17). God is supreme and His power extends to every centimeter of the world.

This isn't good news for boastful Edom. God will exercise His sovereignty among the nations and direct hearts to do as He wills—in this case, to bring Edom down. He's already cued us into His plans to do so through other nations. The battle shout has been decreed to gather the nations together for war against Edom, and the cry originated in none other than God Himself.

God shows us many ways He directs the hearts of nations and people in Scripture. One of the best known is Pharaoh in the Old Testament, whom Moses approached to free the Israelites from slavery. Several times, Pharaoh himself refused to release them, but other times God hardened his heart and the hearts of his servants so He could perform mighty signs and miracles among them (Ex. 10:1). God interjected Himself in the affairs of Egypt just as He plans to do with Edom's enemies. It's doubtful the enemies (like Pharaoh) knew God was using them, but their lack of awareness didn't stop God from having His way.

In this verse, God reveals His plan to bring Edom down from their self-inflated perch of pride. He is about to get their attention and bring them back to reality, and the process will be fierce.

Pride is Avoidable

These verses are packed with applicable action for our lives, and the majority of it centers on the topic of pride. Giving too much credence to our hearts negates the One who searches them. Edom gave themselves way too much credit and paid for it dearly. The consequences of pride may vary, but they are unavoidable when we, like Edom, succumb to the pride that so eagerly waits to entangle our hearts. Fortunately, we can learn from Edom's mistakes before our pride grows enough to necessitate major consequences.

First, we can learn that pride is avoidable. Edom didn't have to yield to pride when their circumstances were pleasant. They could have remained humble and turned to God as their Mighty Fortress instead of trusting in the fortresses of the natural rock that surrounded their dwelling places.

Pride is avoidable for us as well. We are often tempted to compare ourselves with others and take credit for things we have no business claiming as our own merit. Time and again we will be confronted with opportunities to say no to pride and yes to humility, which, by the way, is greatly defined as thinking of ourselves less, not thinking less of ourselves.[XLII] The next time you are tempted to cave to pride, don't compare yourself with someone around you. Instead, compare yourself with Jesus. If His perfection isn't the most effective tool of humbling sobriety, I don't know what is.

Pride is a Mirage

The second truth we can learn from Edom's pride is that any pride derived from physical circumstances is nothing but a mirage. Edom fancied themselves on the clefts of the rocks like eagles perched in their nests, towering high above other peoples around them. What they failed to realize is that, however unlikely, their location could be taken from them. Nothing tangible in this world is secure to the point of being impenetrable. God was about to strip them of their security, yet they refused to believe it because of their false sanctuary in their geographical location. Psalm 20:7 describes this erroneous perspective well: "Some boast in chariots and some in horses, but we will boast in the name of the Lord, our God."

We take pride in the most fickle of circumstances. Athletes boast in their ability to perform physical feats that leave mere mortals in awe. CEOs steward their finances arrogantly and use them to buy the latest and greatest toys in order to appear better off than their neighbors. Housewives and stay-at-home moms pride themselves on the cleanliness of their homes, on the achievements of their children, and on their wardrobes. What these and many others fail to realize is that everything we prize can be taken away as swiftly as an eagle seizes its prey. A single play can injure an athlete beyond hope of ever playing again. A shortcut in a business deal can dismantle the entire kingdom a CEO has been building. The housewife's home can burn to the ground; children can get sick and stray without any satisfying explanation.

Favorable physical circumstances are gifts from God, but they're not guaranteed to last forever. He can continue providing them, or He can take them away, as He did with Job. To take pride in what we have instead of who He is (we are, after all, called to boast in Him) renders us as useless as a mirage of a bubbling fountain in the middle of a scorched desert.

Pride is Blinding

The third lesson we can learn from Edom's arrogance is that pride is blinding to the point of misplacing reality. Edom grew so cocky, they believed they were impermeable—that no one in heaven or earth could bring them down. A dose of common sense would dissipate this view. No one is that powerful or strong. The greatest kingdoms of earth have come and gone, even the ones people thought would last forever.

But that's what pride does. It blinds us to reality by thrusting us in the realm of the alter-ego. Just as it left Edom unable to see the obvious truth, it renders us unable to use common sense and, more importantly, God-sense. When we take pride in things like finances or physical achievements, we inevitably place ourselves on the throne of our lives. When things go well, our egos receive an even greater boost to the point we leave others behind. This stands in stark contrast to God and His way of living.

God calls us to put Him first, others second, and ourselves last. The old saying is true in many ways: Jesus, Others, and You…what a wonderful way to spell JOY. This is the only way we can experience true joy in this life. Pride may give us fleeting happiness, but humility brings us lasting joy. When we trust God and strive to live as He tells us to (according to the gospel), we place ourselves in the best possible position to make the most of our lives here. We may not make as much money, gain as much recognition, or be the envy of the neighborhood, but we will absolutely bring glory to Him and experience a degree of satisfaction we never imagined possible.

At its foundation, pride blinds us into making something else our Savior in place of Christ. We are sick, sinful people who desperately need to be rescued. Pride makes us think we can rescue ourselves, that we can accrue enough resources, status, wealth, power, and security to make us virtuous people and keep us in God's good graces. Nothing could be further from the truth. The only means of genuine rescue comes through the shed blood of Christ on our behalf. He's the One who came to earth, lived a sinless life, suffered and died in our place and for our sins, and rose again the third day to prove His power over death. When we accept Him, we invite Him to be Lord of our lives, which leaves no room for any arrogance on our part. We do nothing to secure our own salvation; we can do nothing to keep it. That's why Paul says, "he who boasts is to boast in the Lord" (2 Corinthians 10:17).

Frankly, there's no room for pride in the life of a Christian, unless we're boasting about our amazing Lord. Instead of dependence on God, Edom chose dependence on themselves. Over time, this manifested into blinding pride that left them devoid of the reality found in God.

Pride Severs Relationships

The last truth we can learn about pride through Edom's story is that it severs our relationships—first with God, then with others. Scripture shows us that Edom had been separated from God for quite a while before Obadiah penned his vision. Generations before, Esau neglected God's gifts and chose instead to satisfy his temporary desires. This pattern persistently marked his life. For years, it no doubt continued in his family and eventually in the nation of Edom. By the time Obadiah writes his vision, Edom is severely disconnected from God. Their pride has blinded them to the reality that He is sovereign and active in the world, which sets them up for the rude awakening they were about to receive. God despises pride, and any arrogance within our hearts is sure to keep our relationship with Him from flourishing (or even existing).

Pride also severs our relationships with others. As stated before, comparing ourselves with others is a natural byproduct of pride. After all, we cannot see how great we are until we notice how lowly others are. This attitude strips any bonds that hold our relationships together. No one likes being around arrogant people, and nothing will make people run away faster than a heart consumed with pride.

Pride comes with consequences. It severs relationships with both God and man. It's a mirage that leaves us trusting in physical circumstances instead of God. It's blinding and causes us to live in the realm of alter-ego instead of the reality God shows us in His Word. But it's also avoidable if we don't follow Edom's footsteps. We can choose humbling dependence on God rather than arrogant dependence on ourselves and our physical circumstances. Which have you been choosing? Does any area of your life need redirection this week?

GROUP STUDY

INTRO

> Pride goes before destruction, and a haughty spirit before stumbling.
> (Proverbs 16:18)

Pride is a cancer that sneaks into our souls and won't stop destroying us until we're consumed and separated from God. It takes many forms, has vast consequences, and is something we all struggle with.

- Share a time when you (or someone you knew) exuded pride about something and were brought low (humbled) because of it.

- In what areas of your life do you tend to struggle with arrogance? Relationships? Your career? Your reputation? Your looks? Etc.

THE WORD

Obadiah's vision is from the Lord, and it brings major charges (and lethal judgments) against the nation of Edom.

> We have heard a report from the Lord, and an envoy has been sent among the nations saying, "Arise and let us go against her for battle"—"Behold, I will make you small among the nations; you are greatly despised" (Obadiah 1:1b-2).

- Who is being called to go against Edom for battle?

    o Who is orchestrating the uproar?

    o What are his plans?

"The arrogance of your heart has deceived you, you who live in the clefts of the rock, in the loftiness of your dwelling place, who say in your heart, 'Who will bring me down to earth?' 'Though you build high like the eagle, though you set your nest among the stars, from there I will bring you down,' declares the Lord" (Obadiah 1:3-4).

- What is the major charge God brought against Edom?

    o What evidence of this charge do you see in their attitude?

- What does God compare them to?

    o Why do you think that's significant?

- Who will bring them down?

    o Why do you think that's significant?

APPLY

The charge of pride has been levied against Edom, and its severity demands direct, divine intervention by God Himself. We can learn several things about pride from Edom's situation. If we're wise, we will apply them to our lives before the pride gets out of hand.

- Pride is a _____

    o What did Edom trust in above all else?

    o Why was that an unwise choice?

    o What do you tend to trust/find security in other than God?

- Pride is _____

- o Edom believed they were impenetrable. How does this perspective show their blindness to reality?

- o Have you experienced a situation in which pride blinded you (or someone you loved) to reality?

- Pride severs _____

  - o Edom's pride severed their relationships with God and others. How did that leave them vulnerable? Why is that ironic?

  - o How do you see pride severing relationships around you?

- Pride is _____

  - o What do you think Edom could have done to keep from traveling down the road of pride?

  - o What steps can you take this week to choose humility instead of pride?

PRAY

Share prayer requests and encourage one another to apply the truths learned this week.

Week Three:
Weak Spots

OBADIAH 1:5-9
PERSONAL BIBLE STUDY QUESTIONS

1. When thieves rob a home, do they usually take everything (1:5)? Why or why not?

   - What items are usually of most interest to thieves?

2. Read Leviticus 19:9-10. Why were the Israelites instructed to leave gleanings in their fields and vineyards?

   - How does this principle complement Paul's instruction in 2 Thessalonians 3:10 on behalf of the poor?

3. What kind of treasures will be searched out within Edom (1:6)?

   - Read Psalm 139:1-16 Can we hide anything from God? Is that a comforting thought to you or an intimidating one? Why?

4. Will any of Edom's friends remain allies with them (1:7)?

- Have you ever felt alone or abandoned? What was the situation? How long did it last?
- Read Hebrews 13:5. Will God ever leave or forsake His children? How does that promise make you feel?

5. Who will God destroy from Edom (1:8-9)?

- Why would losing these particular people be difficult for Edom?
- Who would you consider a source of wisdom and strength in your life?
- What do you think life would be like without such counselors?

COMMENTARY

"If thieves came to you, if robbers by night—O how you will be ruined!—would they not steal only until they had enough? If grape gatherers came to you, would they not leave some gleanings? O how Esau will be ransacked, and his hidden treasures searched out! All the men allied with you will send you forth to the border, and the men at peace with you will deceive you and overpower you. They who eat your bread will set an ambush for you. (There is no understanding in him.) "Will I not on that day," declares the Lord, "destroy wise men from Edom and understanding from the mountain of Esau? Then your mighty men will be dismayed, O Teman, so that everyone may be cut off from the mountain of Esau by slaughter." (Obadiah 1:5-9)

***

Our culture operates from a perspective of fairness. We try to make punishments fit crimes appropriately. If two children are racing but one is much younger than the other, we'll give the younger one a head start to give him/her a chance. In marriage, we compromise to be fair. If one spouse gets to choose the countertops in the remodel, the other may get to pick the carpet. It's all about checks and balances in relationships and the way we operate. We like keeping everyone happy to the best of our ability, and we do it best through the exercise of fairness.

While this is a good principle to apply within a broken culture, it fails miserably in God's economy. Contrary to what people may think, God is not fair; and He never claims to be. Some of us may be nodding our heads in agreement, thinking, "You're right! I went through a terrible tragedy that I didn't deserve. I'm a good person. I tithe regularly and go to church every weekend. Why would God allow something like that to happen to me?" This perspective is understandable and widespread. We see a lot of pain and suffering in the world, and it's easy to blame it all on God and His unbalanced distribution of fairness.

Unfortunately, such a perspective is also grossly skewed. It begins with a huge assumption that's quite false, namely, that we deserve anything good and wonderful in this life. Ouch. Yes, that sounds rather harsh, but hear me out. Because of sin, the only thing we deserve, the only things we have rightly coming to us, are death and hell. Even the smallest sin separates us from God (Romans 3:23), who is holy, true, righteous, and perfect. Since we cannot repair our broken relationship with Him on our own, we should hope for nothing but hell, wrath, and judgment in this life and the next (Romans 6:23). It may not be a popular sentiment, but it's the truth.

If God were "fair," at least as we define fairness, He'd leave us on our own to face the consequences of our sin. But God isn't fair, and that's fantastic news for us! Rather, God is inconceivably unfair. He extends grace where judgment is deserved and mercy where wrath should be found (Ephesians 2:8-9).

His cup of wrath, which we deserved to drink, was consumed by Jesus, the suffering Servant who died in our place (Mark 14:36; Hebrews 2:9). Those who accept Christ stand under the covering of His blood and have been declared innocent before God (Hebrews 9:12, 22). While we will still encounter the consequences of our sin on earth, one day we will be safely nestled under Christ's covering as we stand before God and are declared righteous.

But not everyone accepts this free gift of salvation. This is important to keep in mind as we dive into the next section of Obadiah. God's judgment against them is fierce and comprehensive, and if we're not careful, we might see Him as a bully. He most certainly is not! By the time of Obadiah's vision, He has extended Edom hundreds of years of grace—opportunity after opportunity to turn to Him. Yet they continually reject Him and His gift of mercy. As He does with us, God reaches a point when He will pour out His wrath. He's extremely patient, but His patience has a limit.

"IF THIEVES COME TO YOU, IF ROBBERS BY NIGHT—O HOW YOU WILL BE RUINED!—WOULD THEY NOT STEAL ONLY UNTIL THEY HAD ENOUGH?"

Theft has been around since the beginning of time, even making it into the Ten Commandments. It was a common occurrence in biblical times, just as it is in America today. According to the Federal Bureau of Investigation, well over 8 million property crime offenses (mostly theft) occurred in the nation in the year 2013. That's over 23,000 crimes every single day, 980 every single hour, or 16 every single minute. That's insane!

Needless to say, we are familiar with the concept of theft, even if we've never participated in it. (But who can honestly say they never stole a piece of gum or a dollar out of Mom's purse as a kid?) Just as God employed imagery in the last section, using eagles to help us understand the height of Edom's pride, He now incorporates the imagery of theft to help us understand the vastness of Edom's impending judgment.

The concept of theft is so familiar to us, we miss the fact that it follows a process. First, it involves a thief. Can't have a theft without a thief! Second, it involves an object that doesn't belong to the thief. Objects vary immensely and may not even be physical (i.e., songs can be stolen from the internet). But every theft involves an object that the thief desires but isn't willing to pay for. Next, theft requires a plan. Whether the decision to steal is impulsive or well thought out, at some point, the thief envisions his opportunity. Finally, theft demands action. Without the act of taking something, theft remains merely a plan in the mind of the would-be culprit.

Nothing in this process is foreign to us, and neither is the point that God is trying to make by pointing out a final, obvious fact about theft: thieves never (or hardly ever) take everything. When someone robs a house, he usually takes the most valuable items—electronics, jewelry, etc. He doesn't enter the house and start packing up everything in sight. He chooses what's most valuable and will give him the best return. A family photo album is not typically high on the priority list, whereas an heirloom diamond necklace is.

God's point is that even the most felonious thieves don't take everything from their victims. Something is always left behind.

"If Grape Gatherers Came to You, Would They Not Leave Some Gleanings?"

Here another analogy elaborates on the point. Just as thieves don't take everything when they steal from someone, so grape gatherers wouldn't take everything either. Grapes were one of Edom's staple crops, so this hits close to home.[XLIII] We are much more familiar with the concept of theft than we are grape gathering, so let's take a trip back into Old Testament times to see what God's talking about.

When Israel exited Egypt after 400 years in slavery, they were quite a pathetic crew. They didn't have a lot of skills other than those needed to perform their slave duties. As a whole, they were unfamiliar with agriculture, traveling, military operations, government structures, and so on. Thus, when they finally got to the Promised Land, God had to lay out specific laws for them to follow. One such law involved their harvests, and

He states:

> Now when you reap the harvest of your land, you shall not reap
> to the very corners of your field, nor shall you gather the
> gleanings of your harvest. Nor shall you glean your vineyard, nor
> shall you gather the fallen fruit of your vineyard; you shall leave
> them for the needy and for the stranger. I am the Lord your God.
> (Leviticus 19:9-10)

By not gathering every bit of their harvest, the Israelites helped provide for their poor. Those who couldn't provide for themselves (widows, orphans, etc.) or who had fallen on difficult times would have the opportunity to follow the harvesters of a field and collect what they had left behind. This was a brilliant rule for many reasons. It prompted generosity from the people as a whole, the poor weren't receiving hand-outs (they still had to work for their food and could therefore maintain dignity), and it honored God when His children took care of one another.

You might be familiar with the story of Ruth, who worked as a gatherer during a significant time in her life. When Ruth's husband, brother-in-law, and father-in-law died, she traveled back to Bethlehem with Naomi, her mother-in-law, to start over. They didn't have a means to support themselves since they were both widows, so they relied on Ruth to glean the fields during harvest:

> And Ruth the Moabitess said to Naomi, "Please let me go to the
> field and glean among the ears of grain after one in whose sight I
> may find favor." And she said to her, "Go, my daughter." So she
> departed and went and gleaned in the field after the reapers."
> (Ruth 2:2-3a)

By utilizing the law God had established, Ruth and Naomi could gather enough food to live on. Those who've read the story know that Ruth ends up with far more than just food when she gleans the fields!

The practice of gleaning was familiar to other nations as well, so God's question, "If grape gatherers came to you, would they not leave some gleanings?" was well understood by the original audience. They, like we, understood that both thieves and grape gatherers leave at least something behind. No one would strip a home or field completely bare.

"O HOW ESAU WILL BE RANSACKED, AND HIS HIDDEN TREASURES SEARCHED OUT!"

Unlike the victim of theft and the harvesters of a field, Esau (Edom) will be ransacked, and all their hidden treasures will be searched out. They won't just get robbed of their valuables. They will be stripped bare of everything. The New Living Translation paraphrases this verse well:

> Every nook and cranny of Edom will be searched and looted.
> Every treasure will be found and taken. (Obadiah 1:6)

That's quite the punishment! Not even the smallest crevices of their rock fortifications will be safe from this total plunder. No stone will remain unturned in the pillage; not one inch is safe from the consuming intensity of God.

Nothing can be hidden or kept from God. This truth is either comforting or unnerving, depending on your current relationship with Him. King David was comforted by the fact that God is omnipresent:

> O Lord, You have searched me and known me. You know when I sit down and when I rise up; You understand my thought from afar. You scrutinize my path and my lying down, and are intimately acquainted with all my ways. Even before there is a word on my tongue, behold, O Lord, You know it all. You have enclosed me

behind and before, and laid Your hand upon me. Such knowledge is too wonderful for me; it is too high, I cannot attain to it. Where can I go from Your Spirit? Or where can I flee from Your presence? If I ascend into heaven, You are there; if I make my bed in Sheol, behold, You are there. If I take the wings of the dawn, if I dwell in the remotest part of the sea, even there Your hand will lead me, and Your right hand will lay hold of me. Psalm 139:1-10

EDOM'S MATERIAL DOOM
IN VS. 5-6

RANSACKED =
Pillaged

HIDDEN TREASURES SEARCHED OUT =
Nothing left behind

God's power cannot be contained because He knows no boundaries. He is at once present with kings in palaces and with you in your kitchen, with the wealthy businessman and the swollen-bellied child in Africa. For those in a great relationship with Him through Jesus, this truth is exceedingly uplifting. No matter what we're struggling with or facing on a daily basis, He is there. Even in the moments when we feel utterly alone and abandoned, He is present and availing Himself to us. There's nowhere we can go to fall away from His presence. No sin is so great that we lose access to Him in Christ.

But for those who aren't in good standing with God, His omnipresence is intimidating and unnerving. For them, it means there's no escape. There's nowhere to turn where God isn't there and watching. In other words, there's no privacy from God! He knows every detail of your past—actions, thoughts, words, and hidden motivations. He knows every nuance of your present—where you are and what you're doing at all times. He knows every aspect of your future—nothing escapes His notice.

What could be the most comforting fact in the world then becomes suffocating. *Why can't He just leave me alone?* you wonder. The most basic answer is because He loves you too much to leave you where you are, rotting in sin. Delivery from sin requires that He 1) know about it and 2) take action, which is exactly what He did with us in Jesus and what He did with Edom (though by the time of Obadiah's vision, Edom had rejected His offers of deliverance).

Edom experienced God's omnipresence and sovereignty in a negative way because they refused to acknowledge His blessings and gifts. They claimed self-sufficiency, so God was going to give them an opportunity to test their abilities. They would realize soon enough that they would be laid bare before Him, along with all their earthly treasures.

While total plunder seems like a harsh punishment for the sin of pride, we must remember that it's not unwarranted. Edom had hundreds of years to turn to God and humble themselves before Him, but instead they chose to remain proud. To the degree that pride consumed their hearts, their territory would now be consumed and plundered.

"ALL THE MEN ALLIED WITH YOU WILL SEND YOU FORTH TO THE BORDER"

Winston Churchill once said that the only thing worse than fighting with allies, is fighting without them.[XLIV] Anyone familiar with politics and war knows the power of an ally. Accruing allies when facing a war is one of the most advantageous moves a nation can make. Allies increase a nation's strength, degree of intimidation, resources, and much more.

Like any other nation, Edom had allies throughout their history. We've already discussed how Israel was not one of them, but a nation (especially one as small as Edom) couldn't survive without at least some political friends.

What's particularly interesting about the Hebrew word for "allies" in this text is its weighty definition. Instead of simply meaning a contractual, political partnership, the word *beriyth* means "covenant partners."[XLV] Covenants were a big deal in biblical times and could be identified in one of three ways:

1. A two-sided promise between human parties who both voluntarily accept the terms of the agreement
2. A one-sided disposition imposed by a superior party
3. God's self-imposed obligation, for the reconciliation of sinners to Himself[XLVI]

The type of covenant between Edom and her allies would fall under the first category and would've been taken very seriously. Broken covenants had serious ramifications, but as we'll see, God is not bound to uphold covenants made between humans. Despite the weight of the covenants made with their allies, Edom would be stripped of the protection they offered.

Judgment upon Edom will penetrate much deeper than geography. If it stopped there, Edom would simply be displaced and would need to find a new residence. God's judgment, like their pride, is thorough, and He uses the reversal of their covenant allies to destroy the protection they once thought impenetrable in their geography.

Those allied with Edom will turn against them and send them "forth to the border." This phrase means that Edom's former allies will drive them out of their protective fortresses and toward their borders. In other words, Edom's allies will expose them. Those whom Edom trusted most will render them vulnerable and unable to protect themselves.

"AND THE MEN AT PEACE WITH YOU WILL DECEIVE YOU AND OVERPOWER YOU"

While we would define allies as "men at peace" with us, the relationship between those "at peace" with Edom reaches beyond politics. Those at peace with Edom are their friends and/or those on friendly terms with them in a professional manner.[XLVII] Friendship is far more significant and personal than political ties, for there's a greater expectation of trust. You don't have to secure an official covenant with someone in order to be their friend and expect them to do right by you.

Unlike political allies, friends are close to us. When facing a difficult situation, we can count on our friends to be there. The depth of a friendship can be marked by one person's response to a crisis in the life of the other. If your "friend" shies away when times get tough, you were never true friends. Acquaintances with friendly attitudes, perhaps, but not genuine friends.

Like most of us, Edom had friends they could count on when times got tough. They lived in fortresses and had good friends who had their back. Why shouldn't they feel secure?

Just as God will take away their rocky fortresses and political allies, He will also turn their friends against them. Those they once trusted would soon become a source of great agony—they would "deceive and overpower" Edom. The description of deceit is ironic when we consider what we've learned about Edom. They've already deceived themselves. They allowed pride to grip their hearts so fiercely that they fell into the pit of self-deceit, thinking they were above the reach of both man and God. Now they will be deceived again, not by self-inflicted arrogance, but by those they trusted as friends.

Friends have the power to hurt us deeply, but there's perhaps no greater pain than that of deceit. Have you ever been deceived by someone you trusted? Someone you loved? Betrayal is crippling and damaging, and it casts doubt on all our relationships. We get into survivor mode and tell ourselves we won't get hurt again, so we build walls around our hearts and evict everyone, not just the guilty party.

Edom is about to get a sobering reality check that will wake them up from their arrogant slumber. Their political allies would drive them out of their "secure" land, and their friends would be waiting to deceive and overpower them—leaving them defenseless and helplessly exposed.

"THEY WHO EAT YOUR BREAD WILL SET AN AMBUSH FOR YOU. (THERE IS NO UNDERSTANDING IN HIM.)"

As if losing their geographical advantage, political allies, and friends wasn't enough, Edom will also lose their remaining amiable relationships. The phrase "they who eat your bread" is difficult to translate because in Hebrew the word "eat" was left out, probably by scribal error.[XLVIII] We can safely assume from other references in Scripture (and from history itself) that those who share bread are considered to be on friendly terms.[XLIX] In fact, "eating and drinking together is part of the covenant-making ceremony in Israel and the Near East…so this meaning would well fit the Obadiah context where allies and friends proved unfaithful."[L] Part of Edom's punishment will be to lose comradery with those they shared meals with, presumably their close friends and even family, thus dealing another debilitating blow to their once-enviable status.

Those on friendly terms with Edom will go far beyond social impoliteness, however. They will set an ambush against them! The word "ambush" here can also be thought of as a "trap," though it (like the phrase before) is also obscure.[LI] The Hebrew word is *mazowr* and it is used only once in all the Old Testament. Regardless of obscurity, because of this phrase's poetical symmetry with the two immediately preceding it, we can safely conclude that any such ambush or trap means trouble for Edom.

The last phrase "there is no understanding in him" is also a bit murky. The most probable rendering is that "him" refers to Edom, since they've been the subject of most everything in this vision thus far. Throughout their history, Edom was void of understanding in many aspects of life, and they will no doubt be perplexed by the sudden shift of their friends to foes.

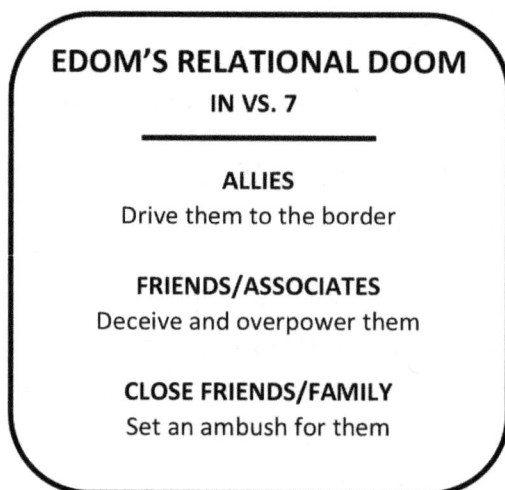

EDOM'S RELATIONAL DOOM
IN VS. 7

ALLIES
Drive them to the border

FRIENDS/ASSOCIATES
Deceive and overpower them

CLOSE FRIENDS/FAMILY
Set an ambush for them

This phrase concludes a trilogy of betrayals awaiting Edom. Their political and national allies will drive Edom from their "protected" hiding places. Then their friends and business associates will deceive and overpower them. Finally, those they share meals with, presumably the closest friends of all, will ambush them. God is striking down their relationships now, which follows a strike on their material goods in the pillage mentioned previously. Due to pride and other sins, they have managed to secure the direct attention of God. Unfortunately for them, it's negative attention full of wrath, punishment, and retribution. Judgment is coming, and it will not be pretty.

"'WILL I NOT ON THAT DAY,' DECLARES THE LORD, 'DESTROY WISE MEN FROM EDOM AND UNDERSTANDING FROM THE MOUNTAIN OF ESAU?'"

God is determined to bring Edom down from "among the stars" of their pride, and the next wave of threats is enough to cripple any nation. On "that day," the day of judgment, God will destroy the "wise men...and understanding" from among Edom's people.

"That day" seems ambiguous but is a well-known concept throughout Scripture. It points to a future time that hasn't happened yet, and in this case, can refer either to Edom's specific day of judgment or the end times, when God's judgment against sin in this world will be final and comprehensive. The immediate context suggests with relative certainly that this "day" will be the one reserved specifically for Edom. Yet, in many ways, it foreshadows the day of final judgment that still remains in the future.[LII]

In the statement, "declares the Lord," God reminds us once again that He is the One speaking. He's made this quite clear, having referenced Himself three times so far, but now He states again that He is the One making these promises of destruction against Edom. His Word brings absolute certainty—there's no way to escape what He promises.

His next threat moves from the general population of Edom's relationships (allies, acquaintances, and close friends) to more specific targets, namely, their "wise men." He promises to destroy wise men from Edom and understanding from the mountain of Esau. Even though this is phrased as a question in the text, it is rhetorical and can be understood as a foregone conclusion.

Wise men in that day were "important figures in the court and society, providing sage intellectual insight or good sense as well as practical skill."[LIII] These are not the kind of men you want your country to be without. They are part of the bedrock of any society, ushering in security through their acts of wisdom and judicial prudence.

Interestingly, Edom had historical ties to wisdom. Job, a wise man, "comes from Uz, which, while unidentified, is associated with Edom."[LIV] Edomites' wisdom is referenced in other passages as well, like Jeremiah 49:7b, in which God asks, "'Is there no longer any wisdom in Teman? Has good counsel been lost to the prudent? Has their wisdom decayed?" (Teman is synonymous with Edom, which we'll see in the next verse). Edom had some kind of reputation for wisdom, which makes this judgment even more intense.

As one who highly values intellect, wisdom, and learning, I consider this one of the most daunting judgments. Our minds are powerful and can be the seats of great wisdom that help us make the most of life and our relationship with Christ. Or they can be seats of great folly that lead us astray. One chilling passage regarding our minds/wisdom is located in Romans 1:20-25a, 28-31a (emphasis mine):

> For since the creation of the world His invisible attributes, His eternal power and divine nature, have been clearly seen, being understood through what has been made, so that they are without excuse. For even though they knew God, they did not honor Him as God or give thanks, but they became futile in their

speculations, and their foolish heart was darkened. *Professing to be wise, they became fools, and exchanged the glory of the incorruptible God for an image in the form of corruptible man* and of birds and four-footed animals and crawling creatures. Therefore God gave them over in the lusts of their hearts to impurity, so that their bodies would be dishonored among them. For they exchanged the truth of God for a lie…and just as they did not see fit to acknowledge God any longer, *God gave them over to a depraved mind,* to do those things which are not proper, being filled with all unrighteousness, wickedness, greed, evil; full of envy, murder, strife, deceit, malice; they are gossips, slanderers, haters of God, insolent, arrogant, boastful, inventors of evil, disobedient to parents, without understanding…

Sin (like pride) corrupts our minds by detaching us from the reality of this world and God's transcending truth. One of the most unnerving things that can happen to us is when God lets us have our way, when He removes His protection and allows our minds to decay in the sin that entangles them. That's what He has planned for Edom. Their wise men, who contributed tremendously to the wellbeing of Edom, would be destroyed.

The word for destroy here is *abad* and means to "perish, vanish, go astray, be destroyed…killed, put to death," and other synonyms for the same.[LV] The exact method of destruction for Edom's wise men is unknown. God could've simply removed the wise men by killing them, or He could've done what He discusses in Romans—giving them over to the depravity of their minds and subsequently allowing them to lose their minds. Through pure speculation, I am inclined to believe the latter. Until this point, God has been promising judgments against Edom that hit them where it hurts most. Allowing wise men to fall into utter foolishness seems far more hurtful (both to the wise men and to Edom as a whole) than merely extinguishing them.

One man in the Old Testament who lost wisdom to the extent that he went mad was King Nebuchadnezzar. He, like Edom, struggled with arrogance. The prophet Daniel warned him to:

> Break away now from your sins by doing righteousness and from your iniquities by showing mercy to the poor, in case there may be a prolonging of your prosperity. (Daniel 4:27b)

A year later, instead of taking Daniel's advice, Nebuchadnezzar grew arrogant and thought his kingdom succeeded because of his impeccable power, glory, and majesty. As he was speaking this to himself,

> … a voice came from heaven, saying, "King Nebuchadnezzar, to you it is declared: sovereignty has been removed from you, and you will be driven away from mankind, and your dwelling place will be with the beasts of the field. You will be given grass to eat like cattle, and seven periods of time will pass over you until you recognize that the Most High is ruler over the realm of mankind and bestows it on whomever He wishes." Immediately the word concerning Nebuchadnezzar was fulfilled; and he was driven away from mankind and began eating grass like cattle, and his body was drenched with the dew of heaven until his hair had grown like eagles' feathers and his nails like birds' claws. (Daniel 4:31-33)

A king became a cow, for all intents and purposes. Nebuchadnezzar traded delicacies for dirt; gourmet food for grass. I can't help but wonder if the wise men of Edom shared this same fate as God continued His trend of complete desolation.

Regardless, the wise men of Edom would be destroyed along with the understanding from "the mountain of Esau." The "mountain of Esau" is a synonym for Edom, referring specifically to Mount Esau. Obadiah seems to be using wordplay here, "playing off Mount Zion (vv. 17, 21) and Mount Seir, a common designation of Edom/Esau, and is a reminder of Edom's mountainous strongholds in verse 3."[LVI] The point remains— Edom's wise men and all understanding therein are doomed for destruction. And it's not over yet.

"Then Your Mighty Men Will Be Dismayed, O Teman, so that Everyone May Be Cut Off from the Mountain of Esau by Slaughter."

In addition to losing their geographical security, allies, friends, and wise men, Edom will now lose their mighty men. In Hebrew, "mighty men" is *gibbowr* and can be translated as "strong man, brave man, or mighty man."[LVII] These men are trained soldiers, the elite of Edom's military and offensive forces.

Scripture contains several references to mighty men similar to those mentioned here in Obadiah. Perhaps the most famous bunch is King David's mighty men described in 2 Samuel chapter twenty-three. These men had quite the reputations and had accomplished insanely impressive military feats. One man, Adino the Eznite, slew 800 men at one time (2 Sam. 23:8). And Eleazar, the son of Dodo the Ahohite, went to battle with David and "struck the Philistines until his hand was weary and clung to the sword, and the Lord brought about a great victory that day" (2 Sam. 23:9-10a). Yet another stood ground against Philistines in the midst of a plot of lentils and kept fighting until God granted him victory (2 Sam. 23:11-12). These three men also traveled behind enemy lines to get water for David simply because he said he was thirsty (2 Sam. 23:15-17).

Are you picturing Herculean-type men? That's probably accurate. Calling these men mighty is like calling an elephant big in light of a flea. They were the absolute top of the military ladder and were an enormous asset to their people.

We don't know how intense Edom's mighty men were, but we can deduce their high value in Edom's military presence. Losing them would be a major blow to an already-destitute Edom, and that's precisely what God has in mind.

The Hebrew word for "dismayed" here is *chathath*, and it carries a sense of being shattered, broken, abolished, and afraid.[LVIII] These soldiers were "called upon to act with valor, but those of Edom are terrified, psychologically demoralized by the catastrophe befalling them."[LIX] Those who once exuded more confidence and bravery than anyone else in the land would shriek and run from their enemies in sheer terror. Instead of defending their people, they would flee and leave them to fend for themselves. The courageous would become cowardly; the daring, daunted, before being ultimately defeated and slain.

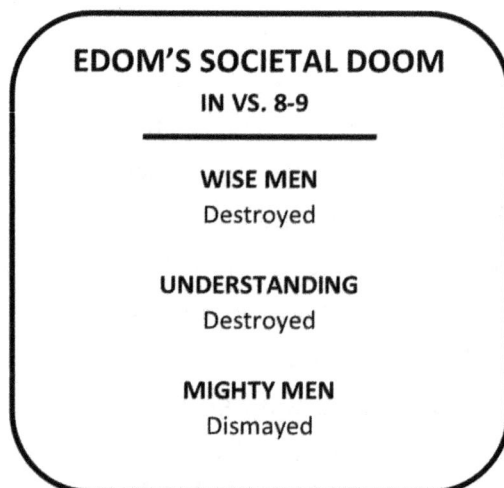

EDOM'S SOCIETAL DOOM
IN VS. 8-9

WISE MEN
Destroyed

UNDERSTANDING
Destroyed

MIGHTY MEN
Dismayed

"Teman" here is used as a synonym for Edom, for it is the name of one of their tribes.[LX] It was also a geographical term, but scholars are uncertain whether it referred to a specific location or just a general area within Edom.[LXI] Nevertheless, the idea is that, with their mighty men cowering in fear and running off, Edom is defenseless, and "everyone will be cut off from the Mountain of Esau by slaughter."

Nothing will stand in the way of God exacting justice on the people of Edom. The "very structures of [Edom's] society, in its constituent elements of economic well-being, wise rule and military security through armed force and international treaty, will topple."[LXII] As His analogy of thieves and grape gatherers makes clear, God will leave nothing behind in Edom. He'll strip them of their material blessings, their amiable relationships, and two major pillars of society: wise men and mighty men. Everything in which they put their security will be stripped away, followed by the people themselves.

Nothing Hidden

Edom's pride blinded them to the fact that nothing can be hidden from God. They thought they were invincible, tucked away in their rocky fortresses, beyond the reach of everyone and everything. They hid their valuables like they hid themselves—behind strongholds they expected never to fail them. This attitude of gross arrogance caught the attention of the Lord on a personal level, and He would soon unleash His wrath upon them in a blur of fury.

The illustrations of the thieves and grape gatherers put a swift end to thinking we can hide anything from the omnipresent God. While thieves and gatherers would leave some loot/harvest behind, God wouldn't. As Edom's arrogance consumed them, so God would consume them—taking every last bit of dignity, worth, and value they had amassed.

While it's unlikely that we'll ever garner God's vengeful attention the way Edom did, we'd do well to remember what they flippantly forgot: God is everywhere all the time; nothing can be hidden or kept from Him. The One who "searches the minds and hearts" can see far beyond what we can, and will give to each of us according to our deeds (Rev. 2:23).

We tend to think we can hide things from God like we can hide from people around us. A man might keep his wife from discovering his affair, but the Faithful One will know. A teenager might use excuses and crafty lies to disguise her addiction, but she cannot conceal it where the Healer won't find it. A single mother may keep the depleted condition of her bank account from those around her, but not from the Provider. When we try to hide things from God, we delay and deny restitution and blessings. God wants to restore, heal, and provide for His children. But unconfessed sin strengthens the walls that keep us from fully engaging in a healthy relationship with Him. The sooner we recognize this, the sooner we can receive healing and enjoy the vibrant relationship He longs to have with us.

The first application point we can make from Edom's demise in this passage is to confess sins we try to hide from God, and from ourselves via self-deceit (like Edom and their pride). Rather than chastising and sentencing us to unpardonable doom, God will use the confession as the starting point of reconciliation. He'll begin to heal us and transform us more into His image (2 Cor. 3:18).

Edom had several chances to turn away from their sin and back to God. Instead, they chose to keep it hidden and allowed their pride to swell. The consequence was a pillage from God more thorough than any mortal enemy could exact on their own. We are faced with the same opportunity—quit hiding what God sees anyway and find healing, or try to cover it up and progress in our suffering and self-deceit. Which will you choose? Will you allow His presence to be a comfort or a concern in your life?

Weak Spots

Another truth we can glean from Edom's impending doom is that we all have weak spots. We all have areas in our lives that we take for granted and would be debilitating if taken from us. Edom thought they were covered and protected. First, they were in a geographically prime location, surrounded by strong natural fortresses and material goods. Second, they had managed to secure relationships with political allies, friends/associates, and close friends/family, and put a lot of weight in the security that came with such covenants. Finally, they had the pillars of their society to lean on—wise and mighty men who could offer guidance and defense as well as improve morale. While none of these security measures are inherently bad, they became weak spots to Edom because they replaced God as Edom's focus and priority.

As with Edom, God tends to strip us of whatever we place ahead of Him in our hearts. He does that in order to regain His rightful spot. Sometimes these weak areas are actually blind spots—we're not aware they exist. When you feel stuck and can't move forward, seek counsel and ask God what the issue could be. You might be blind to the idol you're placing in front of God in your heart and life. But if you seek Him first, He will reveal it to you and help get you back on track.

Others of us are well aware of our weak spots. We're not blind to them at all. Recall Nebuchadnezzar, who prioritized his own glory and wisdom before God's. God warned him about it through Daniel, and when Nebuchadnezzar didn't turn around in repentance, God took away his wisdom and mind, leaving him as useless as a cow grazing in a field for seven years.

Countless modern-day examples highlight this very truth. A man who refuses to tithe, claiming he can hardly make ends meet, sees his money drain from his accounts quicker than he can keep up with it. As soon as he decides to put God first and tithe, God provides and meets his needs day in and day out. Or consider a couple experiencing infertility. They've allowed it to consume their lives and bank accounts, putting it before God. But after working through it and turning it over to Him, they experience peace regardless of the outcome.

The manifestations are limitless, but the principle remains true: when we put something else—anything else—before God, it becomes our weak spot. When God takes it away, it hurts more intensely than we could ever imagine, because we've put our trust and identity in it more than God. God desires and deserves to be Number One in our lives. If He is, our weak spots will dwindle, because our dependence on them has diminished. Will life still throw us hard times? Yes, but they won't be nearly as devastating, because we've kept God first and have developed a lifestyle of trust that will carry us through even the darkest of times.

What's a weak spot in your life? What do you struggle to keep underneath God on your list of priorities? God wants you to learn from Edom's demise and remember that if He's first, you'll be far stronger and able to face life's difficulties head-on, without fear.

GROUP STUDY

INTRO

> "Naked I came from my mother's womb, and naked I shall return there. The Lord gave and the Lord has taken away. Blessed be the name of the Lord."
> (Job 1:21)

No matter how awesome we think we are (or might actually be!), we all have weak spots. These are areas in our lives that, if taken away, would leave us seriously destitute, depressed, and downtrodden.

- Who was Job and what happened to him (Job 1)?

- If you experienced a Job-like situation, in which everything was taken away all at once, what would leave you the most dejected? Why?

- What would you have an easier time letting go of? Why?

THE WORD

As discussed last week, Edom had a pride issue. They put way too much stock in the things of this world and thought their security and identity were impenetrable. Little did they know that a rude awakening would soon leave them exposed and utterly defenseless.

> "If thieves came to you, if robbers by night—O how you will be ruined!—would they not steal only until they had enough? If grape gatherers came to you, would they not leave some gleanings? O how Esau will be ransacked, and his hidden treasures searched out!" (Oba. 1:5-6)

- According to this verse (and life in general) do thieves take everything when they rob a place? What do they typically focus on?

  - How does God compare thieves to the ransacking that Edom will endure?

  - Why do you think that is significant?

"All the men allied with you will send you forth to the border, and the men at peace with you will deceive you and overpower you. They who eat your bread will set an ambush for you. (There is no understanding in him.)" (Oba. 1:7)

- What are the three types of Edom's advantageous relationships described here?

- What will each of them do to Edom?

  - Why do you think that's significant?

"Will I not on that day," declares the Lord, "destroy wise men from Edom and understanding from the mountain of Esau? Then your mighty men will be dismayed, O Teman, so that everyone may be cut off from the mountain of Esau by slaughter." (Oba. 1:8-9)

- Who are the two types of men who will be destroyed/dismayed in this verse?

  - What do you know about them, if anything?

  - Why would their absence pose serious problems for Edom?

APPLY

God is turning Edom's self-professed strengths into dire weaknesses. He plans to cripple them by stripping them of their material goods, amiable and profitable relationships, wisdom, and military prowess. He's going after their weak spots—the spots they've placed in front of Him (unlike Job).

- Have you seen God take someone's top priority away from them (or perhaps experienced it yourself)?
  - What was it like?
  - How long did it take them to get over it?
- What are some ways you can tell if something has replaced God on the throne of your heart?
- What do you need to confess and resubmit to God in your life?

PRAY

Share prayer requests and encourage one another to apply the truths learned this week.

WEEK FOUR:
BROTHER'S KEEPER

OBADIAH 1:10-14
PERSONAL BIBLE STUDY QUESTIONS

1. What is the second reason (in addition to pride) that Edom will face God's judgment (1:10)?

2. Again, how are Edom and Israel related (1:10)?

3. What two punishments will they endure because of their sin (1:10)?

4. How did Edom treat their brother Jacob (the Israelites) in the day of their distress (1:11)?

   • Why do you think this is particularly terrible of Edom?

5. What does God tell Edom not to do in the day of Israel's misfortune, destruction, distress, and disaster (1:12-13)?

We all compare ourselves to others, and many of us find our identity in those comparisons. Do we make as much as he does? Look as good as she does? Have as many friends as they do?

If the answer is "no," we get down on ourselves and grow insecure. If the answer is "yes," (at least, in our own minds) we grow proud and begin to enjoy seeing others fail. If they fail, we feel better about ourselves in comparison.

Take a moment to reflect on this in your life.

- Who do you compare yourself to on a regular basis?
- How do you react initially when they stumble—with concern or a bit of glee?
- Why do you think that is?
- Do you think this honors God? Why or why not?

6. What else does God tell Edom not to do (1:14)?

COMMENTARY

"Because of the violence to your brother Jacob, you will be covered with shame, and you will be cut off forever. On the day that you stood aloof, on the day that strangers carried off his wealth, and foreigners entered his gate and cast lots for Jerusalem—you too were as one of them. Do not gloat over your brother's day, the day of his misfortune. And do not rejoice over the sons of Judah in the day of their destruction; yes, do not boast in the day of their distress. Do not enter the gate of My people in the day of their disaster. Yes, you, do not gloat over their calamity in the day of their disaster. And do not loot their wealth in the day of their disaster. Do not stand at the fork of the road to cut down their fugitives; and do not imprison their survivors in the day of their distress." (Oba. 1:10-14)

***

Once upon a time a man and woman got married and had two sons. One son grew up and became a farmer. He worked the ground and learned all he could about agriculture. The other son grew up to be a shepherd and took care of his family's flocks. Both sons were good at what they did, and both took pride in their work.

One day, they made preparations to bring God an offering. The first son brought the fruit of the ground, and the second son brought firstborn animals from his flock. God accepted the animal offering and was pleased but had no regard for the agriculture offering.

The first son grew angry and his demeanor fell. God noticed, asked why he was angry, and told him that if he did right (obeyed His instructions for offerings), all would be well. He also told him that sin was crouching at the door, desiring to master him. And it would, if he wasn't careful.

God's answer didn't satisfy the first son. Still angry, he decided to tell his brother what God had said. When they were alone together in a field, he rose up against his younger brother and killed him.

God approached the older brother once again, this time asking where his younger brother was. "I do not know," he answered, "Am I my brother's keeper?"

Many of you recognize this story as that of Cain and Abel. These were the first two brothers who ever lived, and their story had a tragic end. Abel, innocent in all respects, died as the victim of the first murder in all of history. His brother, Cain, rashly took the role of the earth's first murderer—someone who caved to sin and allowed his anger, rather than God, to control him.

Sibling rivalry is as old as siblings, and murder is nearly as old as time. Rivalry rarely escalates to murder as it did with Cain and Abel, but it's real and dangerous nonetheless. Likewise, Edom experienced major contention with their brother nation, Israel. Instead of dealing with it and moving on, they let it fester and grow astronomically worse as years wore on. What began as simple sibling rivalry ended up as war between two nations. This too would not end well.

"BECAUSE OF THE VIOLENCE TO YOUR BROTHER JACOB"

So far, Obadiah's vision has been full of damning threats against Edom. All their allies and friends would turn against them, they would be stripped of every material possession. They would lose all their wise and mighty men, which would render them defenseless. The only reason for such grave punishment that we've read so far is their pride. They arrogantly believed they were above everyone's reach, including God's. He despises pride, so harsh punishment for it makes sense. But in this passage, God reveals another item on His list of charges against Edom: their poor treatment of their brothers, Israel.

As with Cain, Edom's rivalry with Israel stretched far beyond quarrels normally seen between siblings. Traditional rivalry between boys involves pranks, tattling, name-calling, and perhaps physical altercations. Most siblings outgrow their rivalry over time and establish somewhat amiable relationships as adults. Others, however, allow the rivalry to fester and never experience healthy relationships with the blood relatives closest to them.

As we discussed previously, Jacob and Esau were brothers and stark enemies. Their relationship was riddled with potholes of deceit, treachery, murder threats, and hatred. These feelings grew with time (one brief reprieve notwithstanding), and they never experienced a harmonious relationship. Unfortunately, their descendants picked up where they left off. Instead of reconciling and living at peace as God intends all siblings (and people, for that matter) to live, they kept at each other and allowed their hatred to stew until it boiled over in battles and wars.

God singles out Edom because of their pride and how they've allowed their rivalry to descend to dire lows. In verse 10, we read that Edom's attitude toward Israel manifested itself through violence—another thing God loathes. God tells us time and again how He is opposed to violence:

> The Lord tests the righteous and the wicked, and the one who loves violence His soul hates. (Psalm 11:5)

> You destroy those who speak falsehood; the Lord abhors the man of bloodshed and deceit. (Psalm 5:6)

> So are the ways of everyone who gains by violence; it takes away the life of its possessors. (Proverbs 1:19)

> Do not envy a man of violence and do not choose any of his ways. For the devious are an abomination to the Lord; but He is intimate with the upright. (Proverbs 3:31-32)

> The violence of the wicked will drag them away, because they refuse to act with justice. (Proverbs 21:7)

> Do not mistreat or do violence to the stranger, the orphan, or the widow; and do not shed innocent blood in this place. (Jeremiah 22:3b)

> "Therefore as I live," declares the Lord God, "I will give you over to bloodshed, and bloodshed will pursue you; since you have not hated bloodshed, therefore bloodshed will pursue you." (Ezekiel 35:6)

> Woe to him who builds a city with bloodshed and founds a town with violence! (Habakkuk 2:12)

Violence has no place within God's family, and it doesn't matter what kind of violence it is. The word for violence in our passage "can indicate both personal physical abuse and practices destructive of institutions and society."[LXIII] In this case it's both—physical and psychological violence by Edom against Israel. They unleash unwarranted, pent-up fury against their brothers and make themselves guilty of yet another sin that God detests.

Viciousness is bad, but Edom's violence was worse because they used it against their "brother Jacob."[LXIV] Jacob here is used synonymously with Israel, just as Edom is used interchangeably with Esau throughout Obadiah. God keeps His writing interesting with synonyms, yet His point remains the same: violence is bad enough when it's against a stranger, but violence done to a relative makes the crime much more evil.

According to the US Bureau of Justice statistics, one in four women has been a victim of severe physical violence by an intimate partner in their lifetime.[LXV] This kind of crime (and other violence involving close relationships) is known as domestic violence. Unfortunately, such violence has touched the lives of millions of people all over the world since the days of Cain and Abel. Edom and Israel grew apart as years dragged on, but they were blood relatives, and that fact doesn't escape God. They, like Cain and Abel, were accountable for their treatment of one another, and Edom is now being called out for their gross violence against their brother nation.

"YOU WILL BE COVERED WITH SHAME"

God was thorough in His description of Edom's forthcoming judgment in the last passage, but a new charge of violence brings new sentencing. First, Edom "will be covered with shame" (Obadiah 1:10b). The word for "covered" in Hebrew carries the idea of being clothed, hidden, or overwhelmed by something.[LXVI] In other words, it's quite comprehensive!

We recently took our dogs to the beach. Both are rescue pups, but that's where the similarity ends. One is a twenty-pound beagle-corgi mix named Tozer (he's a lot cuter than he sounds) and the other is a hound-boxer mutt named Keller, who weighs in at around seventy pounds. Keller is not of fan of water, but since he has paws the size of paddles, we have been trying to pique his interest. Unfortunately, his last experience left him a bit unsettled. We found a spot on the beach for Keller to run around in a little inlet where no other dogs would distract him from his intense game of fetch. Everything seemed to be going great—throw the ball, Keller chases it, gets it, and brings it back while Tozer rolls his eyes. Pretty standard. Until my husband decides to throw it in the water.

Much to our surprise, Keller leaped without reservation into the water to retrieve the ball. Much to Keller's surprise, the water was deeper than any of us knew. Keller got baptized that day—dunked completely under water with a breathy, head-shaking resurrection that will live in dramatic infamy. From then on, the ball had to float back to shore before he would show any interest in retrieving it.

Keller got covered with water that afternoon, and it's the kind of covering God refers to here in Obadiah. Except instead of being covered with water on a sunny day at the beach, God will immerse Edom in shame.

The word for "shame" here is interesting if only because it is unique in the Bible. The Hebrew word is *buwshah*, used only four times throughout Scripture.[LXVII] To an ancient Near Eastern culture, shame was the epitome of despicable descriptions. It stands in contrast with honor, which was held in highest regard in their culture. It's also interesting to compare Edom's pride with their impending shame. Their pride was an internal manifestation of dethroning God in their hearts; but shame is external. Everyone could see it and hold it against them.[LXVIII]

Edom will be covered in shame because of the violence against their brother Jacob, but that's not all.

"AND YOU WILL BE CUT OFF FOREVER"

The descendants of Esau will also be cut off forever—eliminated, destroyed. Shame in and of itself isn't fatal, no matter how much a culture despises it. But being cut off is fatal, and that's the kind of destruction Obadiah has in mind here.[LXIX] God isn't telling Edom they'll be cut off from blessings or an inheritance; He's prophesying their doom. "There is no hope for restoration since there will be nothing to restore."[LXX] "Forever" isn't a synonym for "a while." Edom will be destroyed from this earth forever, never to return. One literal translation of this term "cut off" is for something to be severed, like an amputated leg.

By the time Obadiah penned these words, it was too late for Edom. They were so voluntarily consumed with their sin, it was impossible for them to turn around. We read several similar accounts throughout Scripture: the world right before the flood, the myriads of prophecies against other nations, the accounts of the pagan nations Israel drove out of their Promised Land. God knew the hearts of the Edomites weren't going to change. He also knows our hearts. Does yours have the same prognosis?

While Edom refused, you can repent from your sins and past, turn around, and run toward God. You can exchange despair for delight, shame for satisfaction, and misery for merriment. Your sin isn't oversized enough to keep you from the omnipotent and omnipresent God. His grace is sufficient for you; His power made perfect in your weakness if you'll turn to Him and trust Him. He yearns for you to have a much different fate than Edom. He longs for you to experience eternal bliss with Him through Jesus Christ—to taste His love, to be filled with His peace, and to thrive in His glory.

Edom's punishment does not have to be yours, and it won't be if you learn from their mistakes. They continued in the rut of their sin (which we'll continue exploring next) until it was too late. But you don't have to. What stands between you and God today? What do you need to repent of and allow His Spirit to transform in your life? Is He speaking to your heart with His still, small voice? Listen! And do what Edom refused to do—run hard and fast into the arms of the One who adores you and wants you to bask in His love.

"ON THE DAY THAT YOU STOOD ALOOF"

Now that God has made painfully clear what Edom's future holds because of their pride and violence against Israel, He turns His attention back to the specific ways in which they sinned against their brothers. Our attention turns with His—from forecasting the future to the flashback of facts.

"The day" mentioned here is one that has already occurred. The sin has already been committed, presumably without repentance. We're about to see just how awful Edom was "on the day" and just how guilty they stand before the Almighty God.

First, God charges them with standing aloof instead of taking action when Israel needed them. Delayed obedience is disobedience. The same is true for indifference. Not taking action when you should is the same as contributing directly to the crime.

Our legal system even has a name for this—depraved indifference. This is when "the defendant's conduct [is] so wanton, so deficient in a moral sense of concern, so lacking in regard to the life or lives of others, and so blameworthy as to warrant the same criminal liability as that which the law imposes upon a person who intentionally causes a crime."[LXXI] That's a fancy way of saying that, when someone witnesses or knows of a crime and does nothing to stop it when it is within their power to do so, they are guilty by association and punishable by law.

Edom stands guilty of depraved indifference against Israel by standing aloof when they should've done something. They stood by and watched Israel suffering. God is not letting them off the hook for it.

Here's another way to think about it. Imagine being a modern-day Edom and having a chance to stop the atrocities of 9/11. But because you don't like New York or maybe had a bad experience with a New Yorker, you decide to sit back and let them get what's coming to them. Instead of using your knowledge to act and save them, you stand aloof and let nature take its evil course. Pretty detestable, right? The screams and blood of the children, mothers, brothers, and fathers would be on your hands, just as they were on Edom's with Israel's demise.

"On the Day that Strangers Carried Off His Wealth, and Foreigners Entered His Gate and Cast Lots for Jerusalem— You Too Were As One of Them."

We now learn just how depraved Edom's indifference was against Israel. Israel wasn't just facing a threat of violence when Edom stood aloof. Rather, they were enduring it. "On the day" is repeated from the previous phrase to remind us that we're still talking about past actions, which Edom is standing trial for today.

On the day in question, Edom stood by and watched as "strangers carried off his [Israel's] wealth, and foreigners entered his gate" (verse 11). The "strangers" and "foreigners" are unknown and unnamed, which stands in blatant contrast with Edom ("you"), who is very much known and named. Just in case there's any doubt, God is targeting Edom.

We don't know the identities of the strangers and foreigners. Nor do we know the specific time or instance to which this verse refers. Throughout Israel's history, they were conquered by several different nations. But their identity isn't what concerns God right now. In fact, their identity is entirely moot. Edom is the one on trial, and according to God, they stand just as guilty as the strangers and foreigners who demolished Israel by carrying off their wealth, who entered their gates, and who cast lots for Jerusalem.

While these three crimes against Israel seem tame, they're not, because Israel belongs to God. Any crime against them is a crime against Him. The same is true for us today, though on a slightly different scale. Jesus told His disciples that our actions toward others extend into eternity:

> "Then the King will say to those on His right, 'Come, you who are blessed of My Father, inherit the kingdom prepared for you

from the foundation of the world. For I was hungry, and you gave Me something to eat; I was thirsty, and you gave Me something to drink; I was a stranger, and you invited Me in; naked, and you clothed Me; I was sick, and you visited Me; I was in prison, and you came to Me.' Then the righteous will answer Him, 'Lord, when did we see You hungry, and feed you, or thirsty, and give you something to drink? And when did we see You a stranger, and invite you in, or naked, and clothe You? When did we see You sick, or in prison, and come to You?' The King will answer and say to them, 'Truly I say to you, to the extent that you did it to one of these brothers of Mine, even the least of them, you did it to Me.'" (Matthew 25:34-40)

The way we treat others matters because, as we discussed in Week One, we represent God on this earth. Not only are we supposed to be His hands and feet to people and shine His light to them on earth, we're also supposed to love them, remembering that extending love to them is the same as extending it to Christ Himself.

Israel was attacked by strangers and foreigners as their brothers in Edom looked on and did nothing. Their wealth was carried off, leaving them with few resources of their own. All their wealth had come from God, so the foreigners were robbing Him as well. If you recall from the story of the Exodus, Israel was a slave to Egypt for hundreds of years before God set them free. On their way out, Israel plundered the Egyptians. God had Moses instruct the Israelites to ask their Egyptian neighbors for their wealth, and they complied!

Now the sons of Israel had done according to the word of Moses, for they had requested from the Egyptians articles of silver and articles of gold, and clothing; and the Lord had given the people favor in the sight of the Egyptians, so that they let them have their request. Thus they plundered the Egyptians. (Exodus 12:35-36)

Poverty-stricken slaves became prosperous free people at the expense of their previous slave drivers. The Egyptian plunder sustained Israel through forty years in the wilderness and helped establish them as a nation in the Promised Land. As Israel grew, their riches grew, especially under the leadership of kings like David and Solomon. They would have had nothing without God, so when strangers and foreigners stripped Israel of their wealth, they were stripping them of what God had given them. Not a good idea.

Carrying off Israel's wealth was just the beginning for these strangers and foreigners. Not only did they take what God had given them, but they also breached Israel's security by entering their gates. Gates and protective walls played a huge role in the security of a nation or city in that day and age. Cities without walls (and consequently, gates) were considered vulnerable and easy targets. Enemies could waltz in at their leisure and take over without much of a fight, depending on their strength. So devastating was a lack of walls that it caused Nehemiah great distress when he heard that Israel's capital, Jerusalem, lay in shambles without them:

Hanani, one of my brothers, and some men from Judah came; and I asked them concerning the Jews who had escaped and had survived the captivity, and about Jerusalem. They said to me, "The remnant there in the province who survived the captivity are in great distress and reproach, and the wall of Jerusalem is broken down and its gates are burned with fire." When I heard these words, I sat down and wept and mourned for days; and I was fasting and praying before the God of heaven. (Nehemiah 1:2-4)

Nehemiah understood that a city without walls was like a lone soldier without armor—completely defenseless and exposed. We gather from our passage that Israel (specifically Jerusalem) had walls and a gate, but strangers and foreigners were able to breach them anyway. Such a feat would require a major attack. Edom watched that attack from the sidelines and did absolutely nothing about it.

The last crime mentioned against Israel by their unnamed enemies was that of casting lots for Jerusalem. Casting lots was a common practice in the ancient Near East and was used as "a means of deciding an issue or of determining the divine will in a matter."[LXXII] We don't know the exact methods they used to cast lots, but it could have been similar to rolling dice or flipping a coin today. The outcome determined the verdict or judgment in question, so in this instance, the victor would receive Jerusalem "as a commodity won by the lucky gambler."[LXXIII]

Unidentified enemies surrounded Israel and attacked them, breached their gates, carried off their wealth, and cast lots for the ownership of Jerusalem. They had no regard for God, nor did they respect His people. Edom joined them in their guilt, as we see when God says, "You too were as one of them" (verse 11b). At that point, Edom hadn't physically taken action against Israel. But their lack of defensive involvement rendered them just as guilty as the strangers and foreigners who did attack them.

A quick reminder about sin before moving on. As we discussed in Week Three, our culture's obsession with fairness causes us to weigh everything on our own scales of justness. A child who steals a cookie and confesses quickly gets a much different punishment than the child who deliberately smashes a treasured heirloom vase. We strive to make punishments fit crimes, and for the most part, that works out quite well. After all, it wouldn't make sense for a murderer to serve one hundred hours of community service as punishment while a traffic violator incurred jail time.

This system works well on a horizontal level among mankind. We need rules and corresponding punishments if we're to maintain order in society. But this is not how sin works in God's economy, at least in regard to its effect on our relationship with Him.

In God's eyes, sin is sin. All sin equally separates us from Him. Our white lies do not separate us from God by mere inches while a rapist and murderer is separated from Him by miles. There are no gradations when it comes to our depravity. We are 100 percent depraved because of our sin, yet when we accept Christ as our Savior, we are 100 percent restored (at least vertically) in our relationship with God.

Thus, we have no ground to stand on when it comes to judging God for how He distributes His justice. We can't see people's hearts, but He can. We don't know the depths of sin that encompass others' hearts or if there's any hope of restoration, but He does. Edom stands guilty with Israel's other enemies because of their passivity to the crimes against them, even if they never lifted a finger against them directly (which isn't true, but we'll get there).

God deals with us as He sees fit. The strangers and foreigners would receive due justice as would Edom. We are likewise punished according to His will and our ultimate good.

"Do Not Gloat Over Your Brother's Day, the Day of His Misfortune"

We're about to see how Edom's passivity turns to active participation regarding Israel's destruction. While they may have stood aloof at the beginning, their apathy gradually morphs into action, and they take a more direct role in Israel's demise.

God continues His prophecy against them by telling them not to gloat over their brother's day of misfortune. The present tense of this instruction initially seems misplaced, since the previous two verses make it clear that God is talking about something Edom has already done, not warning them what not to do in the future. Several translations change the tense in order to make it more readable, even though that's not how it reads in the original text.[LXXIV]

To understand the apparent tense discrepancy, imagine God inserting Himself into the past and telling Edom to stop acting so horribly against Israel.[LXXV] It's as if He is recalling a memory so vividly that He's living it out again, telling them not to sin against Israel, even though the crime has already been committed.

Edom's pride is once again brought to our attention. They were passive when strangers and foreigners attacked Israel, and now we learn that they gloated over Israel when they suffered in the day of their misfortune.

Instead of rushing to help, Edom stood back and gloated. The Hebrew word used here for "gloat" is *ra'ah* and traditionally means to look at something intently, though it can also mean to gloat and look down on someone.[LXXVI] This verb solidifies Edom's guilt of depraved indifference. Any suggestion that Edom may not have known about what was happening to Israel is briskly swooped away by their intent and smug gaze upon them. Edom was aware of Israel's dire circumstances, and their pompous glare upon them reflects the pride we've already seen in them.

Once again, Israel is described as Edom's brother, confirming not only their familial connection but also condemning Edom for grossly disrespecting their blood. Brothers may not always be the closest of friends, but they should always be allies. They are family, after all. But Edom's passivity and now gloating disregards any relationship they have with Israel, something God dramatically calls to attention by repeatedly pointing out their blood relation.

Describing the infamous "day" is the Hebrew word *neker*, translated here as "misfortune." This word is rare in Scripture, appearing only one other time in Job 31:3: "Is it not calamity to the unjust and disaster (neker) to those who work iniquity?" The meaning is that of calamity, disaster, and misfortune—all adequate descriptions of Israel's distress at this time in their nation's history.

"AND DO NOT REJOICE OVER THE SONS OF JUDAH IN THE DAY OF THEIR DESTRUCTION"

Edom's smug look upon Israel in their distress swells to the point of rejoicing over their destruction. Instead of realizing their error and changing their ways, Edom escalates in their sin and accedes to its lustful pull.

The word for "rejoice" used here in Hebrew is *samach*. Its definition is rather straightforward: "to rejoice, be glad, make glad."[LXXVII] Edom's merriment at Israel's demise is not slight. They are not indifferent or even mildly amused. They are rejoicing over their brother's doom.

How far does one have to fall in a relationship to get to the point of celebrating when something bad happens to the other? Unfortunately, it happens far more often than we think or would like to admit.

We mentioned before that pride severs relationships by implementing a game of comparison and contrast. When we compare ourselves with people, we're going to end up either above or below them in our minds. If we end up below them, we grow bitter, angry, or depressed. At this point, if calamity befalls them, it brings a sick smile to our faces. When we spend our time comparing ourselves to someone we perceive as "above" us and something bad happens to them, they suddenly seem no better than we are. We may even start to climb above them in our mind's eye. Pride consumed Edom to the point that they rejoiced when others (even their brothers) experienced hardship.

Israel is described here as "the sons of Judah," which could be a slight play on words. Judah means "praised" in Hebrew, which didn't apply to them during these attacks. In seeking praise of their own, Edom belittles Judah, the genuine praised ones, by looking down on them and rejoicing over their tragedy. God will turn it around, however, and will once again raise up His chosen praised ones to their rightful place as His children.

The day of misfortune is repeated with a slight variation, now being called "the day of their destruction." Both refer to the same time but have slightly different emphases. The word for destruction used here is *abad* and is far more common in the Old Testament, used nearly two hundred times.[LXXVIII] It's already been used in Obadiah verse 8—"'Will I not on that day,' declares the Lord, 'destroy (abad) wise men from Edom and understanding from the mountain of Esau?'" Same word, same meaning: to perish, vanish, be destroyed.

Although the same word, the context demands different renderings. When God destroys Edom, it will be total destruction, as evidenced by Obadiah (and that is what happened). But when He speaks of the day of Israel's destruction, it's not as all-inclusive. While Israel's distress will be severe, a remnant will always remain because of God's promise to Abraham and then repeatedly throughout their history:

> "As for Me, behold, My covenant is with you, and you will be the father of a multitude of nations…I will make you exceedingly fruitful, and I will make nations of you, and kings will come forth from you. I will establish My covenant between Me and you and your descendants after you throughout their generations for an everlasting covenant, to be God to you and to your descendants after you." (Genesis 17:4, 6-7)

Israel is God's chosen people; a remnant will always remain, regardless of the intensity of a particular punishment.

One more tidbit to note: Israel was, in fact, punished. They are God's chosen people, but that doesn't mean they are somehow miraculously rid of sin or excused entirely when they do stray from Him. The Old Testament is full of stories of Israel's backsliding ways and their punishment from God. They weren't immune to His punishment any more than Edom or any other nation. He always preserved a faithful remnant, but their suffering was as real as anyone else's.

Of course, Edom should never have been apathetic to Israel's suffering, nor should they have gloated or rejoiced over it. Yet they did, and the condemnation is still coming.

"Yes, Do Not Boast in the Day of Their Distress"

This third phrase marks the end of a rather damning stanza against Edom and their treatment of Israel. God includes another word of emphasis before wrapping up this verse: "Yes." He told Edom that they shouldn't have gloated or rejoiced over Israel's hardship. Before repeating Himself once more, He says "yes" to let us know that everything He's said thus far is good and right, along with what's about to follow.

He once again chastises their pride, telling them not to "boast." The word for boast used here is *gadal* in Hebrew, meaning "to grow, become great or important, promote, make powerful, praise, magnify, or do great things."[LXXIX] This definition doesn't usually have bad connotations. But Edom has a knack for taking good things (like their geography) and making them bad (like the source of unwarranted pride). So it's no surprise that this term is used for them in a negative sense, namely, to act or speak arrogantly against Israel.[LXXX]

The arrogance referred to here is an evolution of the smug look they started giving Israel at the beginning of this verse. Their gloating led to rejoicing over Israel's demise, which fueled their pride until they looked pompously upon Israel in the day of their distress. We are once again reminded that pride blinds us. Edom's haughtiness over Israel blinded them to what God was doing and what He wanted them to do. Instead of recognizing that Israel was God's chosen people and doing whatever they could to help them, Edom swelled with pride to the point of blatant dissent against God. They probably didn't realize how far from Him they were. They sat on their elevated perches, amused at Israel's suffering and completely blinded to the consequences.

Another synonym for Israel's disaster day is used here—"the day of their distress." It likely refers to the same time period and event as the previous two mentions of "the day" in this verse. Yet the word for "distress" here differs from that of misfortune and destruction. The word for "distress" in Hebrew is *tsarah* and means "straits, distress, trouble, or a vexer, rival wife."[LXXXI] Obadiah uses this word one other time in his book (verse 14), but with the exact same phrase, "in the day of their distress." The ultimate meaning remains straightforward: Israel's day of punishment would render them greatly distressed, and Edom boasted about it.

Edom is not impressive in this verse, as we track their slow descent from passive apathy to a growing involvement in Israel's demise. God is mounting charges against them for their attitude and is not finished yet.

"Do Not Enter the Gate of My People in the Day of Their Disaster"

The beginning of this verse (1:13) links it with verse 11 in mentioning gates and entering them. Verse 11 described strangers and foreigners entering the gates of Jerusalem and then casting lots for them while Edom looked on in apathy. Here we learn that Edom personally entered the gates of God's people too. They weren't content to sit on the sidelines and laugh at Israel's demise; they wanted in on the action—cementing their guilt once again in God's eyes (and ours).

Joining with the strangers and foreigners, Edom enters Israel's gates to partake in their destruction. What's interesting is that they are contrasted with the strangers and foreigners. One would expect strangers to have no problem invading an enemy nation and subjecting them to hardship. But we are shocked to hear the account of Israel's brothers doing such a thing. Edom contributes to Israel's temporary doom but might be even guiltier than the others, considering their relationship with their victims.

Heightening the drama of this charge is the fact that God calls Israel "My people." Just as He chews out Edom personally with the use of the pronoun "you" (v. 2, 3, 4, 5, 7, 9, 11, and 12 so far), He uses a personal pronoun for Himself here. By calling Israel "*My* people," God confirms His relationship with Israel and highlights the fact that He is responsible for them and will render justice on their behalf.

We can't help but note a bit of irony between Edom and God and their respective relationships with Israel. Edom is related by blood to the Israelites and thus should have an inherent sense of protection for them and care for their wellbeing. God, on the other hand, has no such intimate connection naturally, but instead has chosen them as His people and, ironically, is far more loyal to them than are their own brethren.

The possessive nature of God's claim on Israel ("My people") continues today. In Christ, we are also His people, "brethren beloved by the Lord, because God has chosen you from the beginning for salvation through sanctification by the Spirit and faith in the truth" (2 Thessalonians 2:13b). During His ministry on earth, Jesus made His connection with others utterly clear:

Jesus insists that those closest to him, those he "owns" as his, those who have ready access to him, those who are part of his real family, are henceforth not his natural relatives, but "those who hear God's word and put it into practice" (Luke 8:21). Unlike many rulers, Jesus showed no interest in a natural dynasty. Nor was his ultimate focus on his tribe, clan, or nuclear family. He came to call into permanent being the family of God—and they are characterized by the obedient hearing of God's word.[LXXXII]

Edom's attack on Israel was synonymous with an attack on God because of His alliance with them. We, too, hold a similar alliance with God if we accept Christ and live in consistent obedience to His Word. Being a Christian today is just as weighty (perhaps even more so) as being an Israelite back in the time of Obadiah. We are God's chosen people and He will absolutely avenge us when someone wrongs us. It might not be as visible as Edom's punishment (before the second coming, anyway), but we can rest assured it will happen.

Now we see another synonym for the day of Israel's suffering. Here and throughout the rest of this verse, God refers to it as "the day of their disaster." The word for "disaster" here is *'eyd* in Hebrew and unsurprisingly means "distress, burden, calamity."[LXXXIII] It's used over twenty times throughout the Old Testament (three within this verse) and is translated almost synonymously each time. Israel will face a time of terrible disaster, and Edom is guilty of contributing to it.

"Yes, You, Do Not Gloat Over Their Calamity in the Day of Their Disaster"

Just in case we're starting to tune out, God gives us yet another word of emphasis. It's directed toward Edom, of course, but He gave it to us to read as well. Actually, He gives us two words of pause and prominence.

The first is a repeated "yes," the same as in verse 12, and the second is another "you," stressing the personal nature of this diatribe.

Sometimes we complain that God is not clear enough. We want to know His will and specific direction for our lives, but sometimes we face tough decisions without any discernable prompting from above. That is most certainly not the case in God's rebuke of Edom in these verses. He uses techniques of interjection and repetition throughout this tiny book to drive home His point—He's the prosecutor and judge in this trial; Edom is the exposed defendant left without an attorney.

Also repeated in this phrase is the word "gloat," which we saw in verse 12. Again, it usually doesn't connote a negative meaning in Hebrew, but it does when used with Edom. Edom smugly looked upon Israel in the day of his misfortune and now does the same in regard to their calamity in the day of their disaster.

THE "DAYS" OF ISRAEL

Verse 12

Misfortune —"neker"

Destruction—"'abad"

Distress—"tsarah"

Verse 13

Disaster—"'eyd"

Verse 14

Distress—"tsarah"

Israel's calamity here is a new word for us, in Hebrew, *ra*. It means "evil, distress, misery, or injury."[LXXXIV] Ancient Hebrew has several synonyms to communicate the same idea (in this case, calamity) just as we do in English. And to give it more flair, God uses many of them in differing sequences throughout His Word. He is quite the expert linguist (being the Author of language and all), and Obadiah seems to be too, as he communicates His message.

From their lofty, rocky perches, Edom intently gazes upon Israel's calamity, their hearts filled with smugness and pride. They are now actively involved in Israel's distress, not just passive observers.

"AND DO NOT LOOT THEIR WEALTH IN THE DAY OF THEIR DISASTER"

After entering Israel's gates and gloating over their calamity, Edom plunders them. God has used the imagery of theft numerous times so far in this book and continues now. First, theft foreshadows Edom's doom—they will be ransacked to degrees that even thieves don't traverse (1:5). Second, theft describes what strangers and foreigners will do to Israel while Edom looks on (1:11). While they won't pillage Israel to the extent that God will do to Edom, they will still strip Israel of the wealth God had given them. Now God mentions theft as an indictment against Edom—they actively participated in stealing from Israel in the day of their disaster (1:13). They stole their wealth, which means they stole from God, the One who gave Israel their wealth to begin with.

One of the most astounding aspects of God's Word is the unity that ties it together. Themes are repeated constantly throughout its pages, revealing God and His gospel in ways we can identify with. While on a much smaller scale, that's what is happening here in Obadiah. Several motifs are used consistently throughout this tiny book, as well as literary devices that make the prophecy not only informative but also beautifully communicated.

The subject thus far hasn't been predominantly beautiful (destruction is hardly attractive), but we can't deny the sophistication and grace with which God communicates. He speaks effectively with elegance, potently with prowess.

Brothers Edom and Israel underwent similar circumstances throughout their histories—times of hardship, times of success, times of plenty, and times of plunder. Israel has had their day of disaster (and would continue to have several in the coming centuries). Now Edom was about to have theirs. But their "day" would be comprehensive and final, not merely a temporary setback like Israel's.

"Do Not Stand at the Fork in the Road to Cut Down Their Fugitives"

The charges against Edom have been fierce: they're full of pride and have actively and passively participated in Israel's destruction. God's also hinted at violence against their brother nation (1:10). At this point, we get our first example of it.

I'm no expert on warfare, but I can imagine when an enemy begins attacking you and you have no resources to fight back, you run. At least, that's what I would do! Apparently, some of the Israelites chose this course of action as well, for when their enemies attacked, some fugitives managed to escape. Unfortunately, they didn't get far.

While trying to escape, Israel's fugitives were cut down by Edomites, who were lying in wait to attack. Since we're unaware of the precise time/event of Israel's "day of distress" mentioned repeatedly in these verses, we don't know what particular "fork in the road" is referenced here. All we can gather is that the Israelites needed to pass that fork in order to escape, and their Edomite brethren waited for them with evil intentions.

Instead of helping their fleeing brothers, Edom lies in wait to "cut down" Israel's fugitives. The phrase "cut off/down" has been used twice so far in Obadiah (1:9,10), both in reference to Edom being destroyed. We mentioned before that karath, the Hebrew word for "destroyed," is not pretty. It means to cut off (like a body part), eliminate, or kill. Thus, Edomites cutting down Israeli fugitives isn't limited to the severing of a political agreement or national alliance.[LXXXV] It means they killed them, most likely by striking them with swords or other such weapons.

Lest we be tempted to glance over this, let's take a moment to contemplate Edom's actions. Looking down on someone with contempt is bad, but this event moves way beyond bad. Smugness regarding Israel has taken so great a hold of Edom's hearts that they escalate to murder—cold-blooded massacre against their kin. No defense attorney could claim self-defense or any other excuse for Edom's actions. They don't just kill; they lie in wait to kill and do so gruesomely. Don't think of a sterile room with a needle, like our criminals receive when they get the death penalty. Don't even think a single gunshot to the head for a quick death. These fugitives bled and suffered—not at the hands of foreign soldiers but of brethren.

People don't just wake up and decide to kill someone. Intentional bloodshed begins in the heart, and it may start with as something as small as pride, as it did for Edom. Jesus made a graphic proclamation about this in His Sermon on the Mount:

> "You have heard that the ancients were told, 'You shall not commit murder' and 'whoever commits murder shall be liable to the court.' But I say to you that everyone who is angry with his brother shall be guilty before the court; and whoever says to his brother, 'You good-for-nothing,' shall be guilty before the

supreme court; and whoever says, 'You fool,' shall be guilty enough to go into the fiery hell." (Matthew 5:21-22)

Sounds harsh, but Christ's words are a scalpel, revealing the intentions of our hearts and where those intentions lead if left unchecked. Edom's pride progressed to smugness regarding Israel, which caused apathy when Israel fell on hard times. This attitude kept a firm grip on their hearts until it spread to their actions. Arrogant thoughts turned into mean thoughts, which led to murder. That is exactly Jesus' point in the passage above. Ill-intentioned thoughts render someone guilty in God's mind; carrying them out is that much more egregious.

"AND DO NOT IMPRISON THEIR SURVIVORS IN THE DAY OF THEIR DISTRESS"

Any Israelites who did manage to survive Edom's ambush didn't have much of a future to look forward to. Again, God would not allow anyone to cut off Israel completely. They were His chosen people, and He would always preserve a remnant. But that doesn't mean the remnant always lived in luxury and never suffered.

In this case, Israeli fugitives who survived their "day of distress" were imprisoned. Whether Edom imprisoned survivors themselves or turned them over to the "strangers and foreigners" mentioned before is unclear, but in the end it doesn't matter. Edom acted against Israel to the degree of no return. They had several opportunities to stop, repent, and turn from their wicked intentions. They could have recognized their arrogance as soon as it sprouted in their hearts and squelched it. They could have realized their apathy toward those they were supposed to love and corrected the issue. But they didn't. At every turn in the road from pride to active violence, Edom pushed forward. They ignored any small voice of conscience (or God) and chose the path most appealing to them, regardless of the consequence to their brothers.

It's Not Too Late for You

By the time Obadiah penned his vision, it was too late for Edom. Their hearts were so far gone and deeply entrenched in sin that it would've been impossible for them to turn back. God knew this (just as He has in countless other instances throughout Scripture) and decided enough was enough. At some point, He will tolerate sin no longer. While this will transpire on a global scale during the end times when He will rid the world of sin, He does so on a smaller scale every day in the meantime. Acts of justice carried out on this earth reflect His heart and will, if only a glimpse of it. Total judgment is coming, yet we should be thankful when we see hints of it in the world around us today.

The fact that you're reading this book and are even remotely interested in spiritual things is cause to celebrate! It is evidence that it's not too late for you to get right with God and experience His grace. Nor is it too late for you to go deeper in your relationship with Him and mature in your faith. It doesn't matter what your past looks like or how old you are; it's not too late!

God is working in your heart to draw you closer to Him, perhaps giving you a glimpse of what awaits you if you choose His path instead of Edom's. Edom had countless chances to repent and spurned every one of them. Your history might be pockmarked with similar actions, but today can be the day you change course. Today can be the day you surrender to God, repent of your pride, and receive His grace instead of His impending judgment.

In Christ, you've already received His grace because Jesus took your judgment on the cross. Why, then, do you continue berating His grace by living in sin (like Edom)? Why keep saying no to the Spirit and remain in your chains when you can say yes to Him and live freely in Christ? It is for freedom that Jesus set us free. Embrace it!

You do not have to repeat Edom's mistakes. In fact, part of the reason we have the book of Obadiah is so we won't. Through Edom's story, God warns us to exercise wisdom and not follow in their footsteps. What started as an internal sin of pride in their hearts manifested into grotesque actions over time, and they scorned every opportunity to correct it. Going through this study could be the wakeup call you need to correct whatever is amiss in your life and threatens to drown your faith. God says that "if we confess our sins, He is faithful and righteous to forgive us our sins and to cleanse us from all unrighteousness" (1 John 1:9). Embrace His forgiveness today by turning from the course you're on and running toward Him. The alternative is destruction, perhaps not as blatant as Edom's, but just as real to your soul and life. The decision is yours: choose wisely!

But repentance from gross sin isn't the only way to take advantage of God's movement in your life. As busy, distracted Americans, we miss out on millions of opportunities to grow closer to God and experience the innumerable blessings He wants to pour into our lives. You could be living at a faith level 4 when He desires you to be a 10. The only thing stopping you (other than unconfessed sin, perhaps), is your awareness of Him and your decision to seek Him above, beyond, and through all the distractions in your life.

Don't put your faith on the backburner as something to deal with "later." Faith in Christ is not merely a get-out-of-hell-free card. Lack of growth may just mean a lack of faith altogether. Seek Jesus now—desire His kingdom and righteousness first, and He'll take care of everything else. Life may not get perfect, but your heart will most certainly soar. The closer you get to Him, the more fulfilled you'll be.

Disasters are Inevitable

As this passage reveals, disasters are inevitable for both the sinner and the saint. Edom clearly had disaster coming, their fate set in stone. But Israel, God's chosen people, also experienced disasters—some of which left them crippled as a nation.

While some disasters are punishments for our actions (let's be honest; we run ourselves into the ground more often than we'd like to admit), others happen to us without apparent rhyme or reason. We are not immune to the brokenness of the world around us. As Christians, we are not of the world. But we are certainly in it for the time being. Thus, while disasters may shock us, we shouldn't be surprised when they occur, because we're not home yet. Peter says it far better than I:

> Beloved, do not be surprised at the fiery ordeal among you, which comes upon you for your testing, as though some strange thing were happening to you; but to the degree that you share the sufferings of Christ, keep on rejoicing, so that also at the revelation of His glory you may rejoice with exultation. Therefore, those also who suffer according to the will of God shall entrust their souls to a faithful Creator in doing what is right. (1 Peter 4:12-13, 19)

This passage echoes Peter and teaches us an important truth in light of inevitable life disasters: God knows what's going on, and He's always with us. In the midst of Israel's despair, God calls them "My people" (Obadiah 1:13). He did not forget or forsake them, even though it probably seemed that way to them during moments of their greatest desolation.

We need to remember this when facing disasters of our own. God tells us:

"I will never desert you, nor will I ever forsake you," so that we confidently say, 'The Lord is my helper, I will not be afraid. What will man do to me?" (Hebrews 13:5-6)

In other words, this world has nothing on us! No matter what Satan throws at us, we can stand confident, knowing God is with us and is working everything out for our ultimate good and for His glory. The next time your life is a disaster zone, meditate on this truth and allow it to flow from your mind until it grips your heart. Revel in God's promises, not your fleeting circumstances. Cling to His Word like the lifeline it is—the anchor that keeps you grounded in faith, even during the worst of storms.

A little addendum for you on this point: having a firm grip on an immovable anchor doesn't keep you from getting drenched in the storm. Disasters still hurt, sometimes fiercely. Losses still need to be mourned, and unfulfilled plans still need to be worked through on a daily basis. Faith doesn't always dull the pain, but it does give it purpose. The fight with disasters isn't primarily an emotional one, but emotions do play a part. So don't get discouraged or be surprised when your hair gets messed up in the storm, even though you're holding onto God and His Word. He'll carry you through and will bring you to the other side. You may look like a mess, but you'll be stronger for it!

Our Brother's Keeper

Just as we aren't immune to the disasters of this world, neither are those around us. We are just as responsible for our responses to others' suffering as we are for our responses to our own. In fact, our reaction to others' suffering not only reveals the condition of our hearts, but we are also accountable to God for it.

Edom didn't understand this. For some reason, they believed that they alone mattered and shouldn't have to concern themselves with the affairs of others—even their own blood relatives. Obviously, God was not pleased with their conclusion, since He implemented a thorough plan of judgment against them for it.

Their perspective is similar to Cain's. When asked about his brother, Abel, Cain responded, "Am I my brother's keeper?" God's answer to this is an astounding "Yes!" We are our brothers' keepers, but who is our brother?

The most literal answer to this question is those related to us by blood. We are responsible for our family members, especially our treatment of them. God has placed them most directly in our path to do life with (at least while we're growing up), so our obligation to them is great. Edom and Israel, of course, fit this category. While they weren't as close during the time of Obadiah's vision, they were still blood, and thus were still responsible their treatment of one another.

But blood relations are not the only ones God has in mind when He speaks of our "brothers" in Scripture. In fact, He uses the term interchangeably with "neighbor," which alludes to any kind of relationship. "Brothers" can also refer to other Christians, those in God's family. But we aren't supposed to treat them with any more respect or love than we do those who don't know Him yet.

The Great Commandment to love God with all our hearts, souls, minds, and strength is followed quickly by a second concerning our neighbors: love your neighbor as yourself. Edom's responsibility for Israel wasn't derived solely from their shared DNA. They had an obligation to them as fellow human beings, people whom God had chosen as His own and had a plan for.

God has surrounded each of us with family, friends, neighbors, coworkers, and more—all of whom are our "neighbors" under God's definition.

When they fall on hard times, God expects us to step up and step into their lives as His hands and feet. If someone falls ill, we should be the first at the hospital to visit and pray over them. When a friend descends into financial hardship, we should help any way we can, even if it means personal sacrifice. While every situation is different and requires discernment, we should never adopt Edom's stance of apathy (and certainly not violence) against the people in our lives.

Are you apathetic toward someone in your life? Someone God might have placed directly in your path to lead closer to Him? Instead, do you show indifference and look the other way? Or, worse—do you look at them with a spirit of pride? Through Edom's downfall, God is telling us that we are our brother's keeper. Take a look at those in your life and figure out how you can be a better keeper this week.

GROUP STUDY

INTRO

> Then the Lord said to Cain, "Where is Abel your brother?" And he
> said, "I do not know. Am I my brother's keeper?" (Genesis 4:9)

While some of us may live like hermits, we are not. God created us for
community and has placed us in specific relationships for a purpose.

- Who were Cain and Abel? What's their story? (Genesis 4:1-12)

- While we may not (and hopefully will never) escalate to murder,
  who in your life (or in your past) do you find difficult to get
  along with? Why?

THE WORD

Edom's pride caused them to think they were untouchable and had no
weak spots. But arrogance wasn't the only reason God would bring them
to their knees in the comprehensive pillage we discussed last week.
Obadiah now makes a turn in his vision that shows us what other charges
God has against Edom:

> Because of violence to your brother Jacob, you will be covered
> with shame, and you will be cut off forever. (Obadiah 1:10)

- What is the new charge God brought against Edom in this verse?

- Why is this a particularly weighty sin?

- What will be their consequences for it?

- Is shame a big deal in our culture? What kind of shame? Why or why not?

On the day that you stood aloof, on the day that strangers carried off his wealth, and foreigners entered his gate and cast lots for Jerusalem—you too were as one of them. Do not gloat over your brother's day, the day of his misfortune. And do not rejoice over the sons of Judah in the day of their destruction; yes, do not boast in the day of their distress. (1:11-12)

- What is happening to Israel (Judah/Jerusalem) in this verse?

  o Who is doing it to them?

- How does Edom contribute to Israel's demise?

  o Why does that make them as guilty as the others in God's eyes?

"Do not enter the gate of My people in the day of their disaster. Yes, you, do not gloat over their calamity in the day of their disaster. And do not loot their wealth in the day of their disaster. Do not stand at the fork of the road to cut down their fugitives; and do not imprison their survivors in the day of their distress. (1:13-14)

- How do Edom's actions in these verses move from passivity to action?

- How do we now see the charge of violence against them being substantiated?

APPLY

Edom and Israel were brother nations by blood. While they may not have remained best friends, they were obligated to care and watch out for each other. But Edom drifted away and grew indignant toward Israel, starting with smirking apathy and morphing into active violence. To God, they were guilty of treason and worthy of the death sentence, which is exactly what they're going to get.

- Read Matthew 5:21-22. How are both apathy and violence toward others the same in God's eyes?

    o How do you think one leads to the other?

- Where do you think apathy/dislike for others can lead in your own relationships?

- Why do you think God cares so much about us getting along?

- Romans 12:18 says, "If possible, so far as it depends on you, be at peace with all men." What can you do this week to live this out?

PRAY

Share prayer requests and encourage one another to apply the truths learned this week.

Week Five:
Investing Wisely

OBADIAH 1:15-16
PERSONAL BIBLE STUDY QUESTIONS

1. What is coming for all the nations (1:15)?

2. Read 1 Peter 4:7. According to it and Obadiah 1:15, when is this day coming?

3. Read Ezekiel 24:14, Jeremiah 21:14a, and Revelation 2:23. According to these verses and Obadiah 1:15, how are the nations going to be judged on that day (1:15)?

   • Imagine standing before God, being judged for everything you have done—thoughts, actions, etc.—for your whole life. How do you think you would feel? What would go through your mind?

4. What will the nations become like when God is finished with His judgment (1:16)?

- We all strive to be remembered, to leave a legacy for future generations. What do you want to be remembered for when you die? When people look back on your life, what do you hope they see?

    o Do you think that will happen based on how you're living right now? Why or why not?

    o What can you change to leave a better legacy in your family, among your friends, in your profession, and/or in this world?

COMMENTARY

> For the day of the Lord draws near on all the nations. As you have done, it will be done to you. Your dealings will return on your own head. Because just as you drank on My holy mountain, all the nations will drink continually. They will drink and swallow and become as if they had never existed. (Obadiah 1:15-16)

***

What comes to mind when you hear terms like "end times," "apocalypse," or "Judgment Day"? Chances are, you see a gruff-looking individual holding a sign on a street corner, demanding that you repent "before it's too late." Or perhaps you think of movies or books like *Left Behind* and envision a time of chaos, disorder, and confusion. While Christians generally agree that there will be a Judgment Day, there's quite a bit of speculation and theorizing about what it will look like and when it will come.

Soren Kierkegaard, a Danish theologian, philosopher, and author who lived in the 1800s, had a theory about what the end of the world would be like. In one of his most famous works, *Either/Or*, he writes:

> It happened that a fire broke out backstage in a theater. The clown came out to inform the public. They thought it was a jest and applauded. He repeated his warning. They shouted even louder. So I think the world will come to an end amid the general applause from all the wits who believe that it is a joke.

Instead of speculating about the when and how of the end times (things we can't know with certainty anyway), Kierkegaard focused on the way he believed some people would respond: with utter ignorance. His chastisement of our ignorance hits its mark. Most of us stand ignorant of the end times in one of two ways: either we push the thought so far back in our minds that it hardly ever surfaces and does not impact our faith, or we speculate to the point of working ourselves into a frenzy and miss the point entirely.

In our defense (as paltry as it may be), few things are as mysterious and unsettling as the end times—the time in which God will judge the world and rid it eternally of sin. This mysteriousness causes us to pass over it and pursue more "relevant" topics like faith, love, and discovering God's will. It's easier to think about what we can see and experience here and now than to contemplate something we don't deem relevant anyway.

What we don't realize, however, is that passing over such a huge part of our doctrine and God's plan hurts us. Kierkegaard knew this and calls us out through his sober analogy. God included several glimpses of the end times for us in His Word, obviously wanting us to know about it and apply what we know to our lives today. If we neglect this (or any other) part of theology, we neglect a portion of our faith and identity as disciples of Christ. History is going somewhere, and God tells us about the destination. We'd be fools to ignore it. If we do, like the theater audience (and Edom), we will only experience our own demise for weeding it out of our faith.

"FOR THE DAY OF THE LORD DRAWS NEAR ON ALL THE NATIONS."

Verse 15 acts as a hinge in Obadiah—seguing the specific judgment pending against Edom with the comprehensive judgment of the nations that will occur during the end times. We can tell it's a hinge verse not only by its content, but also by the use of the word "for" at the beginning. By using "for," a coordinating conjunction, Obadiah wraps up one section and introduces another. In this case, he is going to explain the reason Edom shouldn't have sinned so grievously against Israel.

"The day" has been mentioned already concerning Edom's judgment (vs. 8), as well as in reference to "the day" that Israel was attacked (vs. 11-14). Israel's day of judgment stands in the past while Edom's refers to one in the semi-near future. But "the day of the Lord" mentioned here refers to the day of ultimate judgment—one that will come in the end times.

On this day, "God will defeat chaos and the powers in opposition to Himself."[LXXXVI] Jesus will come back to judge humanity—not to decide where people will spend eternity but to confirm where people have already decided to ally themselves.[LXXXVII] Everyone will be judged, but those who have accepted Christ as their Savior will stand under His grace and will enter heaven; whereas those who have rejected Him will be sent away for eternity apart from God in hell (Matthew 25:31-46).

This is neither the time nor place to fully discuss eschatology—how many judgment phases there will be, the timeline of Christ's coming in regard to other aspects of the end times, etc. The point to capture in our passage, which is reflected in the rest of Scripture, is that there will be a judgment day, and it's coming sooner than we think.

Several times during Jesus' ministry, He talked about being alert and ready for His second coming. Perhaps most famous are His words in Matthew 24:42-44:

> "Therefore be on the alert, for you do not know which day your Lord is coming. But be sure of this, that if the head of the house had known at what time of the night the thief was coming, he would have been on the alert and would not have allowed his house to be broken into. For this reason you also must be ready; for the Son of Man is coming at an hour when you do not think He will."

Peter follows Christ's words by warning us that "the end of all things is near; therefore, be of sound judgment and sober spirit for the purpose of prayer" (1 Peter 4:7). Jesus will come again like a thief in the night. It will take us by surprise and no one will stand untouched by His return.

Many people think Jesus has a funny way of defining "soon," since He spoke those words over two thousand years ago and has yet to return. Obadiah's words were written hundreds of years before Christ, so how could they be accurate? The apostle Peter clarifies this for us in 2 Peter 3:8-9:

> But do not let this one fact escape your notice, beloved, that with the Lord one day is like a thousand years, and a thousand years like one day. The Lord is not slow about His promise, as some count slowness, but is patient toward you, not wishing for any to perish but for all to come to repentance.

God's timing isn't our own, which is a good thing because we are far too impatient. I know I'd have a hard time waiting to unleash ravenous fury on the sin that's consumed this world. I doubt I would've made it past five years, much less a couple of thousand! Yet another reason to be thankful that I'm not God. God's "slowness" in keeping His promise is actually patience. While He sees the sin that overwhelms this world, He also sees us and wants to give us as much time as possible to repent and turn to Him.

But as we've seen in Obadiah and will see one day with the final judgment, His patience has a limit. Edom experienced God's judgment, and "the nations" (i.e., the rest of the world) will too one day.

"As You Have Done, It Will Be Done to You. Your Dealings Will Return on Your Own Head."

As we've seen, Edom will deserve the judgment he will experience (as will all the nations during the end times). Edom's transgressions have been divulged in Obadiah's vision, namely, their pride and violence against their brother nation, Israel. As they have done, so it will be done to them.

The concept of tit for tat or an eye for an eye is not new to Obadiah's readers. God established this principle hundreds of years prior and had Moses pen them within the pages of the law:

> But if there is any further injury, then you shall appoint as a penalty life for life, eye for eye, tooth for tooth, hand for hand, foot for foot, burn for burn, wound for wound, bruise for bruise. (Exodus 21:23-25)

> If a man injures his neighbor, just as he has done, so it shall be done to him: fracture for fracture, eye for eye, tooth for tooth; just as he has injured a man, so shall it be inflicted on him. (Leviticus 24:19-20)

> The judges shall investigate thoroughly, and if the witness is a false witness and he has accused his brother falsely, then you shall do to him just as he had intended to do to his brother. Thus you shall purge the evil from among you. The rest will hear and be afraid, and will never again do such an evil thing among you. Thus you shall not show pity: life for life, eye for eye, tooth for tooth, hand for hand, foot for foot. (Deuteronomy 19:18-21)

These instructions were given to the Israelites to carry out within their own nation. But several times in Scripture, God promises to execute justice accordingly by His own hand:

> "But I will punish you according to the results of your deeds," declares the Lord. (Jeremiah 21:14a)

> "'I, the Lord, have spoken; it is coming and I will act. I will not

relent, and I will not pity and I will not be sorry; according to your ways and according to your deeds I will judge you," declares the Lord God.'" (Ezekiel 24:14)

And I will kill her children with pestilence, and all the churches will know that I am He who searches the minds and hearts; and I will give to each one of you according to your deeds. (Revelation 2:23)

God is the ultimate and perfect Judge; no sin will go unpunished under His reign. That is a truth worth celebrating for those of us secure in our relationships with Jesus! Our sin has been completely forgiven and wiped clean because of Christ's sacrifice on our behalf (Ephesians 1:5-8). We may not see justice executed perfectly during our lives on this earth, but we can rest assured that God is at work and one day "will wipe away every tear from their eyes; and there will no longer be any death; there will no longer be any mourning, or crying, or pain" (Revelation 21:4).

The end times have been delayed so those who haven't yet accepted Christ as their Savior will do so—that they'll repent and accept the grace He extends to them so freely. But as Jesus warns us, we shouldn't let this delay cause us to be apathetic or lazy about His coming. Those of us who are secure in Christ are in the process of running a victory lap before being ushered into God's eternal arms once and for all. But as we run around the track, we should grab as many people as we can. Our lives should move in the direction of His will for the world and His kingdom. Then, when Judgment Day comes, we'll have introduced as many people to Him as possible.

Edom, the nations, and those who refuse to join the lap of victory in Christ will be dealt with according to their sins. Having despised Christ and His gracious gift of salvation, they will stand before Him naked, exposed, and vulnerable—unable to escape the scalding wrath their sins demand.

As we discussed in previous chapters, the consequence of our sin—all sin— is death, decay, pain, and suffering. That's exactly what Edom and the nations will experience on "the day of the Lord" when it finally arrives.

"Because Just As You Drank on My Holy Mountain, All the Nations Will Drink Continually. They Will Drink and Swallow and Become As If They Had Never Existed."

Welcome to the most obscure verse in the book of Obadiah. Verse 16 proves complicated for a couple of reasons: first, because the "you" is ambiguous; and second, because the concept of "drinking" can refer to many things, both literal and metaphorical.

We have three options when assigning the pronoun "you" to someone in this context. It can refer to Edom, the nations, or Israel. Edom would be the obvious choice, since all the obvious second-person pronouns have referred to them thus far in Obadiah. However, when we look closely at the Hebrew, this option poses a bit of a problem. The pronoun "you" used here is "only one of two *plural* forms out of forty second-person forms in the book."[LXXXVIII] The other possible plural form is used when referred to "the nations" in verse thirteen.[LXXXIX]

The next option for "you" refers to the nations. Since the Hebrew word usage matches the plural form used at the beginning of the book, this is a possible conclusion. However, there's a problem with this theory as well. "The nations" referred to in the second half of this sentence are distinct from the personal pronoun. It would be a stretch, then, to assign this personal pronoun to the nations.

Finally, "you" can refer to the nation of Israel. Scholars who hold this view admit that it would be a shocking change of addressee, since Edom alone has been referred to this way thus far in the book. But they think this change is on purpose—"the surprise comes when they [Judah] realize that they, the people of God, are the ones now addressed."[XC] They claim that association with "My holy mountain" (Mount Zion) is much stronger with a subject of Israel as the personal pronoun than with any other option, thus making it the best choice.

While the topic is highly debatable, I'm inclined to agree with option one: "you" is probably synonymous with Edom, since it has referred to them almost exclusively so far in this book. The good news, however, is that we don't have to know the intended subject of this personal pronoun in order to understand the point God is trying to make in this verse: judgment is coming.

This brings us to the second complicated part of this obscure verse, the concept of "drinking." Through Obadiah, God states that just as "you drank on My holy mountain, all the nations will drink continually. They will drink and swallow and become as if they had never existed" (Obadiah 1:16). Our options when interpreting "drinking" here are also three-fold. The first option is literal—the physical act of drinking liquid. The second is metaphorical—the act of drinking representing something else. The third is a combination of the first two—being used literally and metaphorically.

While each option poses some degrees of merit, I lean toward the second option—the "drinking" being metaphorical all the way through the analogy. Throughout Scripture, drinking is used as a metaphor for enduring the wrath of God:

> Let his own eyes see his decay, and let him **drink the wrath** of the Almighty. (Job 21:20)

> Rouse yourself! Rouse yourself! Arise, O Jerusalem, you who have

drunk from the Lord's hand the cup of His anger; the chalice of reeling you have drained to the dregs. (Isaiah 51:17)

Therefore, please hear this, you afflicted, **who are drunk, but not with wine**: Thus says your Lord, the Lord, even your God who contends for His people, "Behold, I have taken out of your hand the cup of reeling, **the chalice of My anger; you will never drink it again**." (Isaiah 51:21-22)

They will **drink and stagger and go mad because of the sword** that I will send among them. (Jeremiah 25:16)

And it will be, if they refuse to take the **cup from your hand to drink**, then you will say to them, "Thus says the Lord of hosts: 'You shall surely drink!'" (Jeremiah 25:28)

You will be filled with disgrace rather than honor. Now you yourself **drink and expose your own nakedness**. The **cup in the Lord's right hand** will come around to you, and utter disgrace will come upon your glory. (Habakkuk 2:16)

And He went a little beyond them, and fell on His face and prayed, saying, "My Father, if it is possible, **let this cup pass from Me**; yet not as I will, but as You will." (Matthew 26:39)

If this holds true in Obadiah as well, God is saying, "Just as Edom drank My wrath on My holy mountain, all the nations will drink My wrath continually. The nations will continually drink and swallow My wrath until they become as if they had never existed."

Edom once drank God's wrath at the hand of Israel, who was headquartered at Jerusalem (Mount Zion or "My holy mountain) then. Both David and Solomon exercised dominion over Edom and punished them because they lacked allegiance to their brothers, God's people (2 Samuel 8:14; 2 Chronicles 8:17-18).

Edom would also drink the cup of God's fury again for their sins against Israel, as highlighted in Obadiah. While God would use other nations to do His bidding, there's no doubt that Edom's judgment came from Him, who aligns Himself with His holy mountain frequently throughout Scripture.[XCI]

Just as Edom did and would once again drink the wrath of God, so would the nations in the final day of judgment. Edom experienced judgment long before the end times (they've been judged and extinct as a people now for hundreds and hundreds of years). But the nations haven't had their final drink of God's wrath quite yet. Their final drink is reserved for the final judgment day.

Thus, it makes sense that the "drinking" referred to here is metaphorical for enduring God's wrath. God promises to give Edom their cup of wrath as He's done before. This also foreshadows the nations' cup of wrath that will follow comprehensively during the end times.

The finality of God's judgment against the nations is enough to make us tremble: "they will drink and swallow and become as if they had never existed" (verse 16b).

My father-in-law recently came to town. As he, my husband, and I drove to dinner, we chatted about an elderly couple in our extended family. The husband had recently taken a turn for the worse in his health. Unfortunately, this couple doesn't know the Lord, nor have they shown even a spark of interest in religion or spiritual matters. Adding to the despair of the situation is their chosen lifestyle—they're practically hermits. They spend time only with each other, having never developed friendships with neighbors or other people in their community. The only communication they have is with family members and perhaps the occasional greeting with a clerk at a grocery store.

As we drove, my husband asked a sobering question, "When he dies, will there even be a funeral? Who would come?" We pondered the question in silence for a moment before realizing that perhaps only a handful of people would come to his funeral. Very few people on earth will be impacted by his passing. How long until he is forgotten? A generation? Maybe two if family photos are kept?

This tragic scenario illustrates the kind of doom Edom and the nations will experience for rejecting God. They will perish to such an extent that it will be as if they had never existed. They will leave no legacy and will be remembered by no one. While God preserves the memory of their demise, He does so ambiguously. We don't see faces or hear names associated with "the nations." We know a couple of facts about Edom, but we don't know enough to be personally impacted by their extinction from the earth.

Our culture equates remembrance with significance, so we strive to do something great with our lives, something that's worth a tribute. Insignificance is terrifying. Having lived without attaining a measure of worth brings anyone to the brink of despair. The only future awaiting the nations and those who reject Jesus is such a fate—existing for eternity in a state of obscurity. God will ensure that they will not be remembered. They will swallow His wrath to the point of fading into endless oblivion.

Are You Living or Existing?

When Adam and Eve disobeyed God by eating the forbidden fruit, they ushered death into the world, not only for themselves, but for every person who would ever live. In a matter of moments, they went from living to existing, from embracing life with God to existing within the throes of death that their sin demanded as a consequence. Because of their sin, we're each born with a sinful nature. Our end is death and eternal obscurity apart from God (Romans 5:12).

Life cannot occur without the Life Giver. Fortunately for us, the Origin of Life breathed hope back into this world through His Son, Jesus Christ. Adam may have ushered sin into this world, and death through sin, but Jesus ushers in the grace of God, which results in justification and life for all men (Romans 5:17). If we believe and accept Christ's gift of salvation (repenting of our sin and allowing Him to reign in our hearts) we can move from existing to living. We can break free from the chains of death and embrace God's gift of life!

We, like Edom, the nations, and Israel in Obadiah's day, have a decision to make. Will we merely exist as time passes, or will we grab hold of the eternal life awaiting us here and now?

Edom and the nations chose existence over living. Of course, they thought they were living. They thought they had it all, and by the world's standards, they probably did—great status, wealth, the ability to indulge in whatever pleasures they wanted, etc. But they were missing something, and it just happened to be the key to life: God. By ignoring Him, they missed out on the genuine life He had to offer. They, like the audience Kierkegaard witnessed, were fools. They were wits who applauded their impending demise, thinking it was a joke.

Many people today adopt Edom's and the nations' perspective on life. They grow satiated with what the world has to offer, to the extent that they've blinded themselves to their need for God. In their minds, Christianity and faith are for the weak; religion is nothing but a crutch to give hope to the helpless who can't fend for themselves. This Darwinian view of life deceives them into thinking they're making the most of life when in reality, they're spinning in circles that slowly spiral to the grave.

The other (far more hopeful) option is to accept God as the Source of Life and embrace His life through Christ as our own. When we accept Jesus as our Savior, we experience an awakening of sorts. It's like waking up from a deep, dreamless sleep. What was most important to us before suddenly doesn't seem as vital in light of the new sights, sounds, and vibrancy we're experiencing. Our goals and dreams may be the same, but the motivations behind them shift. Our priorities change as they align with His, and instead of living for this world, we live as His ambassadors to this world. He gives us a new purpose with our new lives, and we swiftly find ourselves thriving as we never knew possible.

From the moment we are saved, we begin getting glimpses of the eternity that awaits us. In 1 Corinthians 13:12, Paul tells us:

> For now we see in a mirror dimly, but then face to face; now I know in part, but then I will know fully just as I also have been fully known.

While we won't know what heaven is like until we get there, God shows us bits and pieces of what awaits us if we choose to cue into His truth and embrace His eternal life in the here and now. He created us for far more than just existing. In fact, succumbing to mere existence is like slapping Him in the face! We were created in His image to experience life fully and to thrive in communion with Him. He leaves us with the choice of accepting it or not. Edom and the nations didn't. Will you? And not just accepting eternal life once through salvation, but every day seeking to embrace it so we make the most of our lives here on earth?

Investing Wisely

Part of the eternal life God offers us now is the choice to invest wisely. We may have made the transition from existing to living in Christ, but that doesn't mean we automatically invest our thoughts, actions, and time wisely. As God told Edom (and us by extension):

> As you have done, it will be done to you. Your dealings will return on your own head. (verse 15b)

Our sins may be covered by the blood of Christ, but that doesn't mean we're not held responsible for what we do with the life He gives us. Our relationships with Him are secure, no matter what. But the impact we have for His kingdom on earth varies vastly, depending on how we choose to invest our lives.

Edom and the nations never lived beyond mere existing and would pay for it. They chose to invest their lives strictly in things of this world. Judgment day would assuredly reveal the stupidity of that decision.

We, by stark contrast, should invest wisely, making the most of every opportunity God gives us to be used for His glory and the expansion of His kingdom.

Wise eternal investments begin by seeking His kingdom and righteousness first and above everything else in our lives. Jesus explained it well in this parable:

> The kingdom of heaven is like a treasure hidden in the field, which a man found and hid again; and from joy over it he goes and sells all that he has and buys that field. (Matthew 13:44)

If we prioritize His kingdom to that extent, Jesus promises to take care of everything else (Matthew 6:33). We lose the need to worry or grow anxious about what happens in the here and now, because we worship and live for the One who reigns over time forever.

This might sound fine and dandy, but how are we supposed to prioritize Him and His kingdom in our daily lives? When babies scream, bosses make demands, schedules overflow, and time slips through our fingers faster than sand, it's difficult to imagine adding something else, even if it is good.

There's good news for the weary and overwhelmed: the easy and foolproof way to prioritize God above all else isn't necessarily to do more, but to obey more in what you're already doing. God equates obedience with faith numerous times throughout His Word; in fact, obedience is proof that we have faith at all! The apostle John says it well in 1 John 2:3-6:

> By this we know that we have come to know Him, if we keep His commandments. The one who says, "I have come to know Him," and does not keep His commandments, is a liar, and the truth is not in him; but whoever keeps His Word, in him the love of God has truly been perfected. By this we know that we are in Him: the one who says he abides in Him ought himself to walk in the same manner as He walked.

I'm thankful that God makes it easy for us to understand. If we love Him with all our hearts, souls, minds, and strength and love our neighbor as ourselves, we're walking as Christ walked and are being obedient to Him. Obeying just these two commands sets us on the fast track for wise investing for eternity. It may not always be easy to activate in our lives, but with His Spirit, it's certainly possible.

Wise investing, then, means to exercise patience with the screaming babies, work hard and without complaint even under a demanding boss, rework schedules to include rest, and take moments to pause and savor God and how He's working in your life. We invest well when we put Him first in our time, thoughts, and actions—which includes setting aside time to read and study His Word, tithing regularly, praying actively throughout each day day, and treating others the way Jesus did: in love.

Investing wisely is a reworking of our perspective and worldview to match His. It's living for something beyond ourselves and trusting Him to make the most of our obedience. We don't have to be the next Apostle Paul or Billy Graham to make a difference; we simply need to obey Him where He has us. He'll take care of the rest! Take heart and invest wisely by abiding "in Him, so that when He appears, we may have confidence and not shrink away from Him in shame at His coming" (1 John 2:28).

Edom and the nations shrank away to oblivion, and that's often the fate of those who ignorantly think eternal matters aren't relevant in the here and now. But that doesn't have to be your fate. Embrace eternity today through your thoughts, actions, and words. Put His kingdom first and eternal life will be manifested in and through you.

GROUP STUDY

INTRO

> ... Abide in Him, so that when He appears, we may have confidence and not shrink away from Him in shame at His coming. (1 John 2:28)

Very few things are as mysterious and unsettling as the end times or Judgment Day. Lots of theories fly around in churches and religious circles concerning that time, which only adds to the confusion.

- What comes to mind when you hear the phrases "end times," "the apocalypse," and "judgment day"?

- Why do you think it's such a contentious topic among Christians?

THE WORD

As we've seen in Obadiah, the nation of Edom will experience a judgment day of their own for their pride and violence against their brother nation, Israel. But God's message in Obadiah extends beyond Edom's demise to warn us (and the world) about the judgment that awaits the world.

> For the day of the Lord draws near on all the nations. (Obadiah 1:15a)

- What does the "day of the Lord" refer to here? (Hint: look at the Introduction)

- Read 1 Peter 4:7. According to Peter and verse 15 in Obadiah, when is the day coming?

    o Why do you think that's significant? (Matthew 24:42-44; 2 Peter 3:8-9)

As you have done, it will be done to you. Your dealings will return on your own head. (Obadiah 1:15b)

- Who is the "you" referred to here?

- What kind of justice is described?

    o Read Exodus 21:23-25; Leviticus 24:19-20, and Jeremiah 21:14. What do all these passages have in common with each other and with Obadiah 1:15?

    o Why is this manner of justice both comforting and utterly terrifying at the same time?

Because just as you drank on My holy mountain, all the nations will drink continually. They will drink and swallow and become as if they had never existed. (Obadiah 1:16)

- Who is the "you" referenced here?

- What does the metaphor of "drinking" mean in this verse (and/or how is it used throughout Scripture)?

- To what extent will the nations "drink and swallow"?

APPLY

Edom's judgment precipitates the final Judgment Day, when Christ will return and render comprehensive justice to the world. Their fate was destruction because they rejected God, but ours doesn't have to be. Read Matthew 25:31-46.

- According to this passage, who will be judged on the ultimate Judgment Day?

- How will they be judged?

- How does (or should) this judgment impact your life, decisions, and priorities today?

  - This week, how can you invest wisely for eternity, not just for the things of this world as Edom and the nations did?

PRAY

Share prayer requests and encourage one another to apply the truths learned this week.

Week Six:
Full Restoration

OBADIAH 1:17-21
PERSONAL BIBLE STUDY QUESTIONS

1. What will happen to some on Mount Zion (1:17)?

2. Who will stand victorious after the judgment of Edom (1:17-18)?

3. How easy will it be for Israel (Jacob and Joseph) to destroy Esau (1:18)?

4. Will anyone survive from the house of Esau (1:18)?

5. Who guarantees this outcome (1:18)?

    *   Why is that significant?

6. Who will possess the mountain of Esau (1:19)?

7. What will happen to the former Jewish exiles (1:20)?

8. When Esau is judged, who will assume possession of their kingdom (1:21)?

COMMENTARY

"But on Mount Zion there will be those who escape, and it will be holy. And the house of Jacob will possess their possessions. Then the house of Jacob will be a fire and the house of Joseph a flame; but the house of Esau will be as stubble. And they will set them on fire and consume them, so that there will be no survivor of the house of Esau," for the Lord has spoken. Then those of the Negev will possess the mountain of Esau, and those of the Shephelah the Philistine plain; also, possess the territory of Ephraim and the territory of Samaria, and Benjamin will possess Gilead. And the exiles of this host of the sons of Israel, who are among the Canaanites as far as Zarephath, and the exiles of Jerusalem who are in Sepharad will possess the cities of the Negev. The deliverers will ascend Mount Zion to judge the mountain of Esau, and the kingdom will be the Lord's. (Obadiah 1:17-21)

***

Last words are significant. They have the power to alter our moods, change results, and reprioritize schedules. When we read the last words of a novel and they don't tie the pieces together to our satisfaction, we're left annoyed and disgruntled. When we're in an argument with a coworker and they manage to squeeze in the last word before the boss walks in the door, we're left stewing and replay the scenario over and over in our minds—convinced we could have changed things if we'd gotten the last word in. When our spouse informs us at the end of a phone call that our in-laws will be coming for an extended visit...tomorrow, our priorities change for the next several days. When we hear or read about someone's last words before they die, we grow contemplative and evaluate our lives in light of what they learned is most important.

Examples are numerous, but the truth remains: last words are influential, and we're wise to pay attention to them.

We began this study reviewing the weight of words. God chose Obadiah to communicate a specific message to a specific people group. His entire vision consists of less than one thousand words, but he chose each of them deliberately and carefully, accurately reflecting what God had shown him. God preserved them for thousands of years and clearly wants them to impact our lives for eternity today. We are wise to seek, savor, and apply the truth within them.

As the vision draws near its end, we find ourselves lifted slightly off our seats in anticipation of the closing. Obadiah undoubtedly held his breath as the vision concluded, eagerly awaiting any last bits of truth he would receive. This vision indubitably changed his life forever, and I'm sure he hoped it would impact others' lives to great extents as well. As we move into his final words, let's pay close attention to what is said so we, like Obadiah, don't miss the final morsels of truth God has for us.

"BUT ON MOUNT ZION THERE WILL BE THOSE WHO ESCAPE, AND IT WILL BE HOLY"

Always looking for literary cues, we notice right away that this verse serves as another transition in Obadiah because of the conjunction "but." God has pronounced judgment against Edom and predicted a comprehensive judgment day against the nations in verses 15-16, but now He begins the process of fitting together the rest of this vision's pieces.

Both Israel and her enemies (Edom and the nations) have endured punishment and trials in this vision—some of it in the past and the rest in the immediate and distant future. But while Edom and the nations will "become as if they had never existed," Israel would not. True to His Word,

God would keep a remnant of Israelites for Himself, preserving the people He chose for Himself since the time of Abraham (Genesis 17:4, 6-7).

On Mount Zion (synonymous with Jerusalem and Israel throughout the Bible), some of God's people would escape the wrath He was pouring out on the nations. The word for "escape" here is quite interesting, for it communicates more than just an evacuation. In Hebrew, the word is *peleytah*, and it means both escape and deliverance.[XCII] A Jewish remnant isn't merely escaping, then. Rather, God is delivering them through His judgment of their enemy nations.

Lowly Israel now rises above their enemy nations. In Obadiah 1:11-14, we saw how Israel suffered at the hands of Edom—robbed, invaded, gloated over, and severely distressed. Those who managed to escape didn't make it far before being cut down or imprisoned. But that's not the case now. God stepped in and brought deliverance for His people. Those who were once beaten refugees are now the recipients of divine liberation. Israel has experienced enough hardship. God will restore His people to their original position as His favored ones.[XCIII]

The reference to holiness at the end of this phrase ("it will be holy") is a bit difficult to pinpoint because the pronoun "it" is unclear. One interpretation suggests the "it" refers to "a holy place, a sanctuary, a rebuilt temple" that will be placed upon Mount Zion in due course.[XCIV] Another interpretation is probably correct in stating that "it" likely refers to Mount Zion itself, "which is sanctified by the presence of Yahweh (cf. Exod. 3:5; Ps. 11:4) and set apart for his use (Isa. 52:1)."[XCV]

God is in the business of restoration and deliverance as much as justice and judgment. In fact, it's quite difficult to separate His deliverance from His judgment throughout Scripture because one is used to achieve the other. His judgment contributes to our deliverance from sin; the only way to rid someone of sin is to distribute punishment for it (thank God for Jesus, who took the punishment on our behalf!).XCVI Edom rejected God and His salvation, so they would be punished; justice would be satisfied. By executing judgment against Edom, God not only punishes them for their grave sin against Israel, but also avenges Israel for the suffering they endured. Thus, justice is twofold, both a positive (vengeance for the victim, Israel) and a negative (punishment for Edom's sin).

"AND THE HOUSE OF JACOB WILL POSSESS THEIR POSSESSIONS"

Part of any restoration process is gaining back what has been lost. When a theft takes place, restitution demands that the loss be compensated, either by equal monetary value or a replacement of the item stolen. The same principle applies to a host of other examples. An injured athlete might have surgery in order to be restored to their sport in a healthy way. Compromised relationships might need counseling in order to experience restoration. Restoration cannot occur without some kind of reinstatement of what's been lost, even if it doesn't look exactly the same as before.

Israel's restitution and restoration will be no different. They endured a severe marauding at the hands of their enemies, and now they would take back what was stolen. The "house of Jacob" refers to Israel as a whole. God changed Jacob's name to Israel and used it interchangeably the rest of his life (Genesis 32:28). Jacob's descendants experienced the same use of synonyms throughout their history as well.

Another way to read the phrase "possess their possessions" is to interpret it as "reclaiming their inheritance." Again, Israel contributed nothing to their success or wealth. God supplied them with riches when they left Egypt and continued adding to them as they slowly took possession of the Promised Land. All their material possessions originated with Him, so when they repossess their goods and/or inheritance, they merely gain back what had been given them before.

When God restores, He does so completely. What had been stolen from Israel would be returned to them at the great expense of Edom's (and other nations') demise. God may allow temporary tribulation against His people, but in the end, He restores His people fully.

"Then the House of Jacob Will Be a Fire and the House of Joseph a Flame; But the House of Esau Will Be as Stubble. And They Will Set Them on Fire and Consume Them, so that There Will Be No Survivor in the House of Esau," for the Lord Has Spoken.

God's restoration of Israel won't stop with the mere return of material goods. Just as part of any restoration process is the replacement of what was lost, so also is enduring punishment and the consequences of the offender's actions. A thief must not only replace what was stolen, but he must also be punished for his theft (i.e., time in prison, a fine, etc.). The same is true for Esau. Not only will they be stripped of what they took from Israel, but they will also be punished severely for taking it in the first place.

The "house of Jacob" here is juxtaposed to the "house of Joseph," which forces us to do some clarifying. While both refer to Israel, God is getting a little more specific by separating them into two separate entities. After King Solomon's reign, the nation of Israel split into two kingdoms: the northern kingdom and the southern kingdom. The northern kingdom became synonymous with Israel and Joseph, and the southern kingdom became synonymous with Judah and Jacob. All of Israel is still referenced with these two identities. God just seems to be using a clever literary technique of repetition to create more textual interest.

Both "houses" of Israel will become like "a fire and…a flame" that will consume their enemies. The imagery of fire is new for Obadiah, but it fits the previously mentioned motif of comprehensive judgment well. God promised to ransack Esau and search out all their treasures (vs. 6). The imagery of fire serves well to illustrate the process by which that will happen. Just as a fire consumes everything in its way, so will God consume Edom with judgment.

The next part of the verse reveals that the task won't be too difficult. The "house of Esau" (Edom) isn't as fortified as they think.[XCVII] They aren't some kind of concrete structure that can put up a fight against or delay hungry flames. Rather, they are as "stubble" or chaff—easily consumed by the flame of a candle, much more by a roaring wildfire of God's retribution. Such "tinder dry conditions of a harvested field are familiar to the audience, and the effect of a fire is undoubtedly well known, so the image is immediately appreciated."[XCVIII]

Israel couldn't stand up to Edom much in the past, but now "they will set them on fire and consume them, so that there will be no survivor of the house of Esau" (vs. 18). God will direct winds of vindication Israel's way to help them devour Edom to the point of utter destruction. Not one person will be left from the house of Esau. God's patience has reached its limit.

The totality of this judgment is sobering. Not one single person will be left in Edom, which includes men, women, and children alike. God has distributed acts of wrath like this in the past, but familiarity doesn't make it any less daunting.[XCIX] Psalm 111:10a states that "the fear of the Lord is the beginning of wisdom." God isn't a grandfatherly figure with a jovial chuckle at the prospect of His enemies. He is an omnipotent warrior whose enemies disintegrate before Him. A bit of renewed fear of Him in our hearts would bode well for us, I think. We revere what we fear.

A little side note: I fear for the American church today. We bend over backward to make people feel comfortable instead of convicted. Buildings have stages, flashing lights, smoke, and special effects. Preachers use props and videos and encourage people to sip their white chocolate mochas as they listen. No need for Bibles when paraphrased passages can light up a screen. While there's nothing inherently evil about these individually, the culmination of it all leads to a spirit of irreverence. When we exchange awe of God for theater seating, we have a problem. But I digress.

God doesn't want His children to be afraid of Him (1 John 4:18). But it's healthy to meditate on His unlimited power and perfect justice against sin every once in a while so we stand that much more in awe of Him.

Once again, God reiterates that He is the One speaking, using His name to close this prophetic section "as shown by the switch from poetry to prose in the next verses."[C] This hasn't been a prophecy from a fortune teller, nor was it some literary hocus pocus. It has been God's Word, and His Word is sure—just as secure and powerful as He is! He's assured us three times so far that He is the Author of this message (vs. 1, 4, and 8) and declares His involvement once more. The spoken word of God isn't something to be ignored or taken lightly. It will surely come about precisely as He predicts and commands, as it has every other time in recorded history.[CI]

THEN THOSE OF THE NEGEV WILL POSSESS THE MOUNTAIN OF ESAU, AND THOSE OF THE SHEPHELAH THE PHILISTINE PLAIN; ALSO, POSSESS THE TERRITORY OF EPHRAIM AND THE TERRITORY OF SAMARIA, AND BENJAMIN WILL POSSESS GILEAD.

Now that the verbal prophecy directly from God is complete, Obadiah concludes the recount of his vision with prose, most likely describing what he saw in his vision rather than what he heard as a direct quote from God Himself. This conclusion reveals the crusade of God's judgment against

Edom by giving us a mile-high view of what would happen. It begins with a geographical overview of people's movements.

First, the people of the Negev will move to possess the mountain of Esau. The Negev is "the dry southland of Judea" and adjacent to Edom.[CII]

It should be noted that the mountain of Esau "is the only territory among those listed that is not included within Israel's traditional territorial boundaries (Deut. 2:4-5)."[CIII] That fact implies that God is not only restoring to Israel what originally belonged to them, but He is going above and beyond by adding Edom's territory to their own. Just as Edom went above and beyond normal atrocities when attacking Israel (their brothers), so Israel would do when exacting retribution on Edom.

Next we see the Shephelah possessing the Philistine plain. The verb phrase "will possess" is missing from this phrase, but it is implied since it is linked to the first phrase which does include it. "Shephelah" is also translated "the foothills," and it is Israelite territory located east of the Mediterranean in a perfect position to move against the Philistines. The Philistines were longstanding enemies of Israel (Judges 10:11; 1 Samuel 4:2; 2 Samuel 5:24; 1 Chronicles 10:1). While they wouldn't perish completely like the Edomites would at this time, they would receive harsh judgment and await their ultimate demise around 330 BC. [CIV]

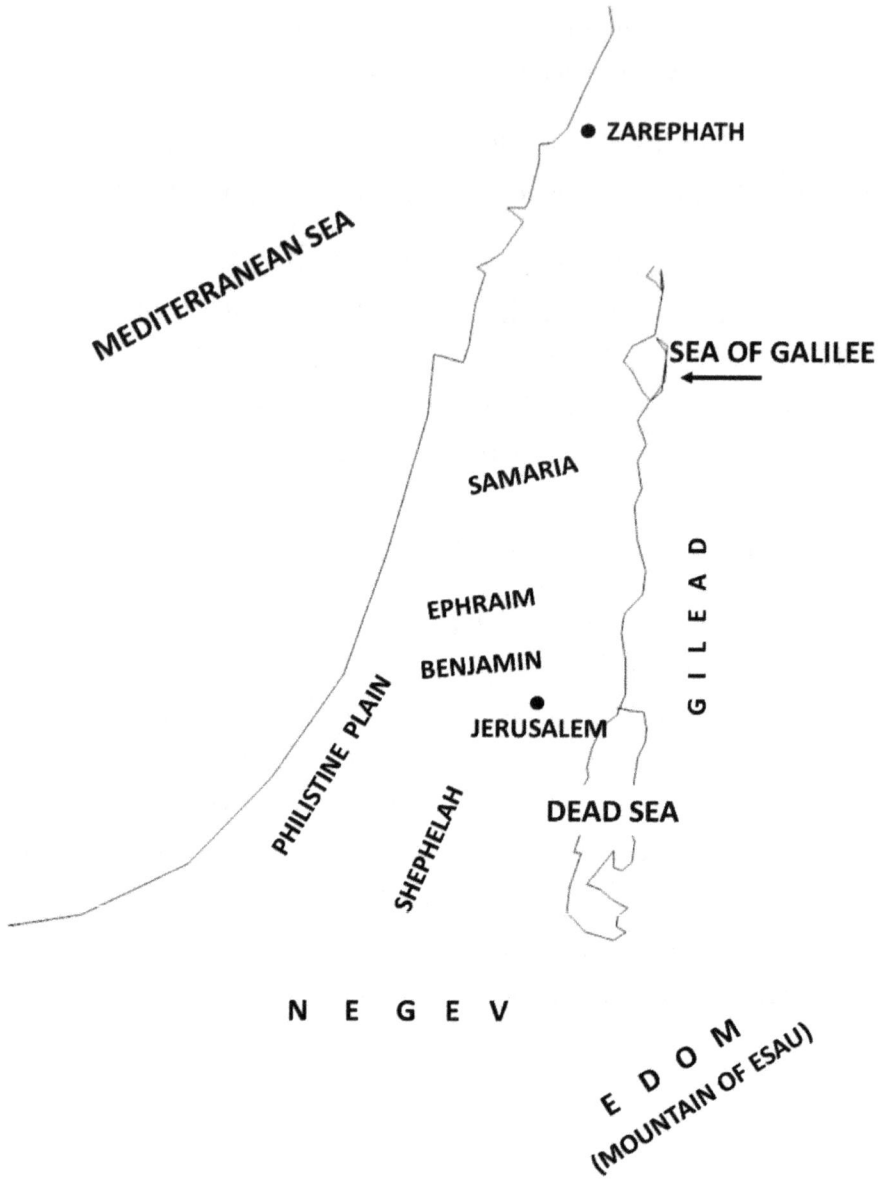

MEDITERRANEAN SEA

● ZAREPHATH

SEA OF GALILEE ⟵

SAMARIA

EPHRAIM

BENJAMIN

PHILISTINE PLAIN

SHEPHELAH

● JERUSALEM

G I L E A D

DEAD SEA

N E G E V

E D O M
(MOUNTAIN OF ESAU)

RED SEA ⟵

Thirdly, we notice a movement to possess the territory of Ephraim and the territory of Samaria. We're not told who will possess these territories, but it's safe to assume that it will be Israel, since they have been the subjects of the aggressors so far. Both Ephraim and Samaria are located farther north than the previous territories and had formerly belonged to Israel, as they were about to once more. Samaria was the Northern Kingdom's capital conquered by the Assyrians in 722 BC. [CV] The group of people who remained became their own nation. The Jews chastised the Samaritans for heretical worship practices. The Samaritans existed as a people group for quite a while longer (we read about them in the New Testament).

Lastly, in this verse we're told that "Benjamin will possess Gilead." Benjamin and Gilead have quite the history together, as seen in a couple of dominant narratives in the Old Testament. The first connection we see between the two is in a sordid story captured in Judges 21. The tribe of Benjamin got into a fight with the rest of Israel and was defeated mightily—only 600 Benjamites survived. Israel grew depressed over their rash war with Benjamin and schemed desperately to find women for the survivors so Benjamin wouldn't die off as a tribe of Israel. The problem was that in the heat of battle plans, the Israelites had taken a vow not to let their daughters marry Benjamites. In the middle of their brainstorming, someone realized that Jabesh-Gilead (a particular region of Gilead) hadn't participated in the vow, nor did they fight against Benjamin. As punishment, Israel attacked Jabesh-Gilead and killed everyone except 400 virgins that could be given to the Benjamites as wives.

A second account of friction between Benjamin and Gilead is found when "Saul, a Benjamite, defeats the Ammonites on behalf of Jabesh-Gilead" (1 Samuel 11:1-11).[CVI] This connection isn't nearly as fierce but still serves to illuminate the brief connection that Benjamin and Gilead shared. Obadiah reveals that Benjamin will take possession of Gilead, reclaiming the region for Israel once and for all.

While it's easy to get lost in the details of geography and history, the theme of restitution and restoration is the intent of this verse. We're blessed to get details of how it will happen (at least, in part), but the priority here is to realize that God is restoring to Israel what He had originally promised them (and then some). They went through times of trials and hardships, but in the end God would bring it all back together. He would have the final say for His people.

AND THE EXILES OF THIS HOST OF THE SONS OF ISRAEL WHO ARE AMONG THE CANAANITES AS FAR AS ZAREPHATH, AND THE EXILES OF JERUSALEM WHO ARE IN SEPHARAD WILL POSSESS THE CITIES OF THE NEGEV.

This verse stands in direct competition with verse 16 for the most difficult verse to interpret in Obadiah. The difficulty in interpretation is of a slightly different nature, though. Verse 16 was tough because of the drinking imagery and identifying the personal pronoun "you." Verse 21, however, is a linguistic mess in the original Hebrew. A literal rendering from the Masoretic Text would read:

> "Now the exile(s) of this army/fortress are for the Israelites who
> are Canaanites as far as Zarephath, and the exile(s) of Jerusalem
> who are in Sepharad, they would possess the cities of the
> Negev."[CVII]

As I said, not the easiest verse to translate, much less make sense of. A brief overview of canonical history may well explain what could've happened to cause this puzzle of a verse. About forty men wrote the books of the Bible, as God inspired them. We don't know how He inspired them to write, only that He did, and every word they wrote down was perfect, true, and right. These manuscripts are the only ones that were 100 percent inerrant, infallible, inspired, and the living words of God.[CVIII]

Over time, each manuscript was copied and eventually translated. The scribes, or copiers of Scripture, were very thorough and took their jobs seriously. But that doesn't mean their work was without error (they're still human, after all!). Translators had an even more daunting task. Languages are vastly different. It's impossible to translate perfectly and without variation. The Bible has been copied and translated into hundreds of languages over thousands of years. A miniscule number of textual discrepancies crept their way into the pages of Scripture. None of these discrepancies impact the theology presented in Scripture, however. They are strictly limited to spelling and grammatical inconsistencies.

Chances are that this verse contains a textual incongruity from being copied and translated for thousands of years. Even something as small as "a minor textual corruption of one misread letter plus a change in letter order could have led to this from an original."[CIX] In other words, as little as two microscopic scribal errors could have produced the chaos that we read in the original Hebrew version of this verse.

The good news, though, is that even in its jumbled state, this verse doesn't threaten the theological inerrancy or infallibility of Scripture. The most likely meaning is that Israel would inherit "Canaanite territory that was at the far north of their original inheritance, balancing the far south of the Negev."[CX] Another commentator agrees that "what is of primary importance for the passage, however, is not the starting point but the destination of the returnees. They come back to the ancestral holdings of Israel."[CXI] God's prophecy of Israel's restoration would come to fruition, even if we're not sure precisely how the components of this verse fit into that plan.

With that rather unsettling introduction, let's see what we can learn from this verse and what scholars have figured out about the people and places.

Israel and Jerusalem are familiar to us at this point, and in this verse are exiles. Their exile status could be referring back to verse fourteen of this prophecy. There we learned that when Israel was under attack from Edom and other nations, some escaped as fugitives and survivors, making them exiles. Israel's exile status here could also refer to a more official exile at the hands of the Babylonians or Assyrians during another time period. Regardless, the Israeli exiles mentioned in this verse will end up possessing the cities of the Negev.

Another people group we read about is the Canaanites, specifically those who occupied the territory as far as Zarephath. Canaan "was one of the old names for Palestine, the land of the Canaanites dispossessed by the Israelites."[CXII] These were people whom Israel drove out of the Promised Land, yet still lingered in several geographical locations throughout history. Their land was vast, encompassing many smaller people groups, yet we can safely deduce that one such location was Zarephath, located far north of the Sea of Galilee (refer to map).

Zarephath isn't completely unfamiliar to avid Bible readers, for it was the city where Elijah found refuge from the famine he announced against the Canaanite god, Baal (1 Kings 17:8-24). Those who originally heard this prophecy would link Zarephath to God's deliverance and domination over the Canaanite god(s).[CXIII]

The last geographical location mentioned in this verse is Sepharad, which remains a complete mystery, since it's mentioned nowhere else in Scripture. Scholars have suggested numerous locations for it, including Spain, North Africa, western Media, or Sardis in western Turkey.[CXIV] As long as we're speculating, I'm inclined to think Sepharad was located somewhere south, since Zarephath was so far north, thereby giving us a swooping geographical image of God's full restitution. If so, Sepharad and Zarephath would serve as bookends to a large expanse of land that Israel would receive possession of. That's total conjecture, but the point remains that Israel is going to get back a lot of the land that was taken from them.

Exiles would become heirs once again. God's people would be restored in numerous ways, including geographically.

THE DELIVERERS WILL ASCEND MOUNT ZION TO JUDGE THE MOUNTAIN OF ESAU, AND THE KINGDOM WILL BE THE LORD'S.

God's restoration for Israel includes punishing their enemies and restoring their material wealth and real estate. Now that we know what will happen, we get a glimpse of how it will come about. A group of "deliverers will ascend Mount Zion to judge the mountain of Esau" (Obadiah 1:21).

These "deliverers" remain unidentified, but the concept is familiar. The Hebrew word used here is *yahsa*, and it means "to save, give ease."[CXV] Most often, this title is used by God to describe His role as Deliverer and Savior to His people (Psalm 106:21, Isaiah 43:3, 11; 45:15, 21; 49:26; 60:16; Hosea 13:4; etc.). But it also refers to people God chose for the specific task of saving His people (2 Kings 13:5). Obadiah's vision leaves out the identities of the deliverers who would take an active role in the fulfillment of God's prophecy, but then again, their identities don't matter nearly as much as the identity of the One who sent them: God.

By ascending Mount Zion, the deliverers once again stake a claim over the capital of Israel in Jerusalem. If you recall from verse 11, Jerusalem had been breached, robbed, and cast lots over during Israel's day of distress. Attacking any city would've been bad, but these enemies (Edom included) went after God's holy city—the one set apart for Him and the epicenter for His people. Yet God has the final word for His Mount Zion. He would send deliverers to ascend and liberate it from foreign rule, then use it as the location by which they would judge Edom ("the mountain of Esau").

We'd be remiss to ignore the play on mountain imagery occurring in this verse. Mount Zion is deliberately juxtaposed with the mountain of Esau, and the winner of the matchup isn't in question. Deep irony is found when we sweep back over Obadiah's vision to verses 3 and 4 and recall the heights of Edom's pride. Edomites lived within rocky fortresses elevated high above their enemies in their geographical mountains. This height in topographical location led to soaring heights of arrogance, and God promised, "though you set your nest among the stars, from there I will bring you down" (vs 4b). God is now bringing them down and doing so via the influence of another mountain—His mountain—Mount Zion. Deliverers would ascend His mountain and, as judges, initiate His reign.

Judging is also a familiar concept in Scripture, both in reference to God (Genesis 16:5, Exodus 5:21, 1 Samuel 24:15, Ecclesiastes 3:17) and those He ordains as judges to rule on His behalf (Exodus 18:13, Judges 3:10, 1 Samuel 7:6). The offices of delivering and judging merge beautifully in the book of Judges as God raises up men and women to serve in both capacities among His people. Consider the first judge, Othniel, whom "the Lord raised up [as] a deliverer for the sons of Israel to deliver them" (Judges 3:9). Othniel not only delivered Israel from their enemy, Cushan-rishathaim, but he also judged Israel for forty years. The deliverers in this Obadiah passage seem to fulfill a similar role—both as deliverers and judges for Israel.

Liberating Israel came with the side benefit of conquering Edom and subsequently judging them. Edom would pay for the way they treated Israel (ultimately by extinction), and their land and resources would be governed at the discretion of the deliverers God appointed on Mount Zion.

Both verse and book conclude with a powerful statement: "the kingdom will be the Lord's" (vs. 21b). This "kingdom" includes far more than geographical latitude and longitude. It "refers to the act of ruling and the status of one as king."[CXVI] While God is technically already the Ruler of the earth and everything in it, He doesn't always exercise His dominion forthrightly. Sometimes He withholds His hand and allows people to entertain their free will, even if it means digging themselves into pits of sin.

Yet for Israel's deliverance from Edom, God will sovereignly step in and take full control of Edom, the nations, and His people Israel. Just in case these people "consider themselves independent, they are reminded who has actual control."[CXVII] God inserts Himself within the affairs of kingdoms, and He makes it painfully obvious that Israel and every other kingdom belongs to Him.

God is Faithful

We are finite people with limited perspectives. Our minds are full of biases, preconceived notions, and expectations derived from our upbringing, experiences, personalities, and more. We are capable of perceiving only one or two points of view at a time, and even then, we are limited in our scope. Consider the Grand Canyon. We are capable of seeing only parts of the Grand Canyon, and even then from only one vantage point at a time. We can move and see another perspective, but we're incapable of seeing the whole Grand Canyon from every perspective at any given moment. We're limited, and while that's not a bad thing, it's necessary to understand when it comes to our faith.

Our finiteness makes it impossible to fully understand and know an infinite God. How can a creature fully comprehend its Creator? How can clay understand how the Potter is shaping it while it still spins on the wheel?

Fortunately, God realizes our vast shortcomings and helps us compensate for them by showcasing different aspects of His nature one bit at a time. He yearns for us to know Him (1 Timothy 2:4). He makes that possible by revealing His characteristics through stories, analogies, metaphors, and more in His Word.

One attribute we learn about Him in this passage (and the whole prophecy) is that He is faithful. While this vision might seem like nothing more than a foreboding message of doom and gloom on the surface, we can dig a little deeper and discover that the doom and gloom is happening because God is faithful. He isn't punishing Edom because He's bored or simply because He can. His punishment is an act of faithfulness—first to His own sense of justice, then to His Word, and finally to His people.

He is faithful in exercising justice over sin. While He is perfect and incapable of sin, we are not. In order for us to experience communion with Him again, He needs to deal with the problem of sin that keeps us from Him. Ultimately, He did this through Jesus—He loved the world enough to send His only Son to die on our behalf so that those who would believe in Him wouldn't perish, but have eternal life (John 3:16). God faithfully steps in and takes our place so we can spend eternity with Him.

But not everyone accepts Christ as Savior and the forgiveness of sin that He offers. God is therefore forced to deal with the sin of those who aren't covered by Christ's blood. He wouldn't be perfect or just if He let sin go unpunished. Edom and other unrepentant nations rejected Him, so God had to punish them in order to remain faithful to justice. Sin will be punished and paid for, if not by Christ, then by the offender.

God is also faithful to His Word and people. When God chose Abraham to be the patriarch of Israel, He made a covenant to protect and secure Israel as His chosen people. Israel has a long history of backsliding, complaining, and failing to uphold their promises (as do we; let's be honest), but not once has God ever forsaken them. He definitely allows them to experience trials as punishment for their sinful ways, but He always preserves a remnant and has to this day.

Anyone who's been in a relationship with God for any period of time can attest to His faithfulness, not just as a historical fact within the pages of Scripture, but personally in their individual lives. I have witnessed this attribute at work numerous times within my own life, as well as in the lives of those around me. I've seen Him answer prayers in miraculous and unexpected ways, heal the hurting, mend shattered relationships, provide financially in hopeless situations, and more. His faithfulness isn't just a nicety, it's a fact of life, as sure as the air we breathe. Israel experienced His unrelenting faithfulness over and over, through Edom's downfall and countless others. How have you experienced His faithfulness? Is there a situation in your life right now that needs an extra dose of His faithfulness? Bring it to Him and let Him take over and shine!

Limitless Omnipotence

Another of God's attributes displayed brilliantly in this passage is His omnipotence—His power and rule know no end. Take a moment to read back over all the locations of our passage and/or look at the map. God's intervention isn't confined by borders, nor is it halted by mortal dynasties. His power extends into every crevice of the earth, even those once thought impenetrable, like the clefts of Edom. He directs hearts and armies according to His will, and when He decides to intervene, He doesn't stop until His plans are fully realized.

Edom could go nowhere to escape God's omnipotent hand of justice. There was nowhere they could hide, run, or fight back that would even stall His judgment, much less combat it. He turned the powerful into the powerless and the forceful into the futile.

This is beneficial to remember when picking sides in this life. As it stands, God and this world are at odds with one another. God warns us: "Do not love the world nor the things in the world. If anyone loves the world, the love of the Father is not in him" (1 John 2:15). Thus, when choosing our allies, we'd be wise to take God instead of what may appear successful and appealing around us.

The descendants of Esau chose poorly. Instead of aligning themselves with God and His people, they partnered with nations who were opposed to Him. They paid the ultimate price for it. Despite hundreds of years of opportunities to turn around and repent, they remained stubborn and obstinate, so they endured the painful side of God's omnipotence.

Who have you aligned with—the puniness of this world or the power of God? Do you trust in what you can see physically over what He's proven true in His Word? Will you bet on the muscle of this world or the might of the One who created it?

God doesn't need us, but we sure need Him. Don't be like Edom and shun the one who wants to save you. Turn around and exchange your futility for His force of strength and power!

Restoration is Full in Christ

We can see some of God's wonderful attributes in this passage and the book as a whole. But we should also take note of a truth that is near and dear to His heart: restoration. We've discussed the problem of sin and our need for salvation, but Obadiah reveals something about our restoration to God that many Christians miss. His restoration is comprehensive.

God promised to restore Israel, not just by giving them back what had been taken, but by executing vengeance on their enemies and expanding their borders geographically, politically, spiritually, and influentially among the nations. By stating that the kingdom would be His, God reveals that the kingdom would be Israel's as well because they belong to Him! His restoration for them is total, complete, and thorough, and He offers the same to us through Jesus Christ.

One of my favorite passages about Christ's role in our restoration to God is found in Colossians 1:17, 19-23a:

> He is before all things, and in him all things hold together. For it was the Father's good pleasure for all the fullness to dwell in Him, and through Him to reconcile all things to Himself, having made peace through the blood of his cross; through Him, I say, whether things on earth or things in heaven. And although you were formerly alienated and hostile in mind, engaged in evil deeds, yet He has now reconciled you in His fleshly body through death, in order to present you before Him holy and blameless beyond reproach—if indeed you continue in the faith firmly established and steadfast.

Christ's sacrifice on the cross made it possible for us to be reconciled and fully restored to God. Our sins have been washed away, removed as far as the east is from the west (Psalm 103:12). But just as He didn't stop at removing and punishing Israel's enemies, His restoration doesn't stop at the removal of sin from our lives. He wants us to experience full reconciliation, and the benefits that come with it are limitless.

Like Israel, we are His children, heirs of His grace with a full inheritance of blessings in Christ (Titus 3:7). We are also given the blessing of the Holy Spirit as a seal and promise to keep us for Himself (2 Corinthians 1:21-22). Also like Israel, we are His ambassadors (2 Corinthians 5:20) to this world, and He promises help in carrying out His mission (Luke 12:11). We are given a new purpose, identity, and peace in our reconciled status (Romans 5:1). Nothing can separate us from His love (Romans 8:35-39). In Christ we are given everything we need to live with full assurance of salvation and hope that comes through faith (Hebrews 6:11). We are promised a special place in heaven, a place that Jesus is preparing for us right this minute (John 14:2). Christ also guarantees access to God whenever we want, because He is our everlasting Mediator (1 Timothy 2:5).

These components of restoration through Christ barely scratch the surface of the myriad that exist for those who call on the name of the Lord and are saved. Israel experienced a brutal day of disaster, but the glory of their restoration dulled the bad memories. That's the kind of future that awaits us in heaven—it will be so glorious that this life will seem dull, monotonous, and nearly irrelevant in comparison. History is going somewhere, and for Christians, it's straight to God in heaven! We may experience grave circumstances in this life, but we have access to full restoration in Christ—not just salvation from sin, but a robust life now and bursting hope in an inconceivably magnificent future.

Are you missing out on the fullness of what Christ has to offer us through reconciliation with Him? Are you taking advantage of only one or two benefits when He yearns to immerse you in all of them? Jesus promises that "whatever you ask in My name, that I will do, so that the Father may be glorified in the Son" (John 14:13). Nothing brings more glory to God than when we embrace His grace and gift of restoration to Him. If you're having trouble experiencing it, start by asking Him to reveal it to you.

As you ask, make sure you're doing so with a pure heart, full of love and gratitude for Him. Jesus also says that if you love Him, you will keep His commandments (John 14:15). He's not a magic genie who exists to distribute wishes. He's our Creator and Sustainer, who wants to give us life! As you ask for wisdom, busy yourself with obedience. Don't let the enemy rob you of what's yours in Christ by distracting you with things of this world. Edom fell for it, but you don't have to.

GROUP STUDY

INTRO

> Let us hold fast the confession of our hope without wavering, for
> He who promised is faithful. (Hebrews 10:23)

An unfortunate reality of life is that it's not perfect. We may experience mountaintop moments that leave us in awe and wonder, but valleys or plateaus always follow, leaving us craving more.

- If you could change/fix anything in your life right now, what would it be? Why?

- What do you look forward to most about heaven? Why?

THE WORD

God has made His stance on sin clear in the tiny book of Obadiah, promising divine retribution against Edom (and other nations in the future) for their sin. But His message isn't only of doom and gloom...

> "But on Mount Zion there will be those who escape, and it will be holy. And the house of Jacob will possess their possessions. Then the house of Jacob will be a fire and the house of Joseph a flame; but the house of Esau will be as stubble. And they will set them on fire and consume them, so that there will be no survivor of the house of Esau," for the Lord has spoken. (Obadiah 1:17-18)

- Who are the ones who escape (cf. verse 14)?

- What word picture does God use to describe the reversed role between Israel and Edom?

  o Why do you think that's significant?

- What is Edom's ultimate destination?

  o What does that reveal to us about God?

Then those of the Negev will possess the mountain of Esau, and those of the Shephelah the Philistine plain; also, possess the territory of Ephraim and the territory of Samaria, and Benjamin will possess Gilead. And the exiles of this host of the sons of Israel, who are among the Canaanites as far as the Zarephath, and the exiles of Jerusalem who are in Sepharad will possess the cities of the Negev. (1:19-20)

- Do any of these places look familiar to you? Which ones? What do you know about them?

- Why do you think God includes all these locations? What do they tell you about Him?

"The deliverers will ascend Mount Zion to judge the mountain of Esau, and the kingdom will be the Lord's" (Obadiah 1:21).

- What two mountains are being compared/contrasted?

  o Why do you think the imagery of height is significant (cf. verse 3-4)?

- At the end of this prophecy (and time in general), who will reign?

  o Why is that good news for us?

APPLY

Justice against Edom is only part of the story in this book. God also shows us His justice for Israel and how He plans to restore them above and beyond where they were at the "day of their disaster." He wants the same for us. When we accept Christ as Savior, God begins a work of restoration in our hearts to reconcile us fully to Himself and to the future that awaits us in Him.

- What are some benefits of becoming a Christian, both in this life and the one to come in heaven? (Titus 3:7, 2 Corinthians 1:21-22, 5:20; Luke 12:11, Romans 5:1, 8:35-39; Hebrews 6:11, John 14:2, 1 Timothy 2:5, Revelation 21:4, etc.)

- Which ones have you experienced a lot?

- What do you wish you experienced more of?

- Read 1 John 5:14-15 and John 14:15. According to these verses, what can you do this week to take advantage of the full restoration God offers you in Christ?

PRAY

Share prayer requests and encourage one another to apply the truths learned this week.

Conclusion

"What in the world?"

"I have no clue what's going on."

"Why are we studying this?"

"How are we going to study this for six weeks?"

I hope the questions that began this study have been answered beyond what you could've imagined. Turns out Obadiah isn't as obscure, mysterious, and worthy of collecting dust as we thought! This intense prophecy spoken by an anonymous man packs quite a punch. Through it, we've discovered truths, not only about an extinct nation, but about God and how He yearns for us to embrace the life He offers.

WE REPRESENT GOD; WHAT WE SAY AND DO MATTERS

The first truth we learned in our study is that we, as Christians, represent God on this earth. We are His ambassadors, and everything we do and say matters greatly. Although we don't know much about him, Obadiah was a man God chose to relay a specific message to the world through a prophecy about Edom. He proved his faithfulness to God by obeying

Him, writing down God's words exactly as he saw and heard them. Obadiah recognized that it wasn't his vision to convey, but God's. This realization spurred a great commitment in his heart to represent God the best he knew how—obeying Him and getting out of the way so others could get as clear a view as possible.

People are watching us whether we realize it or not—our families, friends, coworkers…even clerks at the grocery store. Either we use our words and actions to draw others closer to God, as Obadiah did, or we stand as hindrances, pushing them further away. God has given us the ministry of reconciliation and a powerful little tool called our tongues. Are you using your life to carry out His mission of reconciliation on earth? Do your words and actions reflect our perfect, infallible God or your imperfect, fallible self? Obadiah made a wise choice. We can too!

Perspective is Important

Our study reminded us of another truth: perspective is important. Unlike Obadiah, the nation of Edom held a faulty perspective of God, life, and all its components. First, they lacked proper perspective in their self-identity and pride. Because of their geographical advantage and temporary elite position over other nations, they puffed themselves up with pride to the point of deceiving themselves. They believed they were invincible, even to God. Their arrogance caused them to lose perspective and to detach from reality.

From their failure in this area, we learned some facts about pride: it is a mirage, it is blinding, it severs relationships (with both God and man), and it is avoidable. We do not have to follow in Edom's arrogant footsteps. If we are careful, we can catch seeds of pride and squash them before they take root in our hearts and grow to enormous heights. When we join John the Baptist in saying God must increase, and I must decrease, we realign our perspectives with truth and set ourselves up for a far more satisfying life (John 3:30).

The second way Edom failed to maintain a God-honoring perspective was in thinking they could keep things from Him. At the height of their pride, they believed they were untouchable and had no weak spots. They relied on their strong living arrangements, allies, friends, wealth, and societal structures more than God. Those became the exact targets God destroyed.

We all have weak spots—things in our lives we grow dependent on more than God. When we replace God on the throne of our hearts with anything else, there's a good chance He'll remove it so He can regain His proper place. He yearns to eradicate our weak spots by shining His strength through them, and does so if we'll let Him (2 Corinthians 12:9).

Thirdly, Edom lost perspective when it came to their relationships, specifically with their brother nation Israel. Like Cain, Edom didn't think they bore any responsibility for their brothers. They allowed calloused hearts of apathy to morph into brazen hands of violence and bore the blood of their brothers on their hands.

Our Heavenly Father cares deeply about the way we relate to one another. He created us in His image and for community, and we're supposed to care for, lift up, love, and encourage one another. Next to loving Him, loving each other is the most important thing we can do in this life—the second greatest commandment He gives us (Matthew 22:39). Edom failed to uphold this perspective, and the result wasn't just a lack of relationship. It was gruesome violence. When we fail to love others, we descend a slippery slope. Apathy can easily transform into anger and can destroy relationships. Anger can easily morph into violence or other devastating actions, reaping major consequences for everyone involved. The moral of the story: align your perspective of relationships with God's. It may not always be easy, but it's always worth it.

Lastly, Edom neglected to maintain a healthy perspective of eternal matters. They lived as though this earth were their final destination and refused to acknowledge that any day of reckoning would ever befall them. As God states in His prophecy, there will be a judgment day, not just for Edom but for all nations.

It may not be a happy topic to think about, but one day we will all be judged for our actions, words, thoughts, and deeds. Some of us will stand under the cover of Christ's blood, forgiven and justified. Those who have rejected salvation, however, will stand guilty before God and incur His full wrath for eternity. God's perfect justice demands that sin be atoned for, either through Christ or by our suffering in hell. Edom chose the latter; we certainly don't have to do the same!

Wisdom calls us to realize that our choices now bear eternal significance. We invest in eternity whether we're aware of it or not. Let's choose to invest wisely in the kingdom that awaits us, not foolishly like Edom.

Edom's perspective was skewed in their pride, weak spots, relationships, and eternal mindset. They lost sight of what was important and replaced it with the temporary because it was more appealing. Satan would like nothing more than for us to do the same. We have one life on this earth. How we choose to live will determine our circumstances in eternity. Keep this perspective and life will be much better for you where it counts—with peace now and unending blessings in heaven to come.

GOD IS IN THE RESTORATION BUSINESS

In Obadiah, Edom's downfall is only one part of the big picture, which is God's plan to restore Israel. Bringing restoration and hope to Israel involved judgment for Edom's sin, because restoration cannot occur without the guilty being punished and justice being served. But Israel wasn't just avenged for their suffering. They were blessed and reconciled fully as God's people. God restored their land, wealth, and status beyond what they originally had, and He's working to do the same for us too.

God has begun a movement called the gospel. Among other things, it is a movement of restoration. He is restoring this world to Himself through Christ and making preparations for a new heaven and earth without the mar of sin. While we may not experience the full ramifications of this restoration in this life, we can embrace overwhelming benefits here and now.

Christ paid the penalty of our sin so we could stand forgiven and then experience the magnificent inheritance God offers us, His children. Unfortunately, we often neglect the benefits we have in Him. Even simple blessings like peace, joy, contentment, encouragement, and hope elude us, partly because of our ignorance of their existence and also because of our refusal to ask for them.

God wants to fill our lives with His blessings now, not just when we get to heaven. This doesn't mean life will be perfect or He'll make us rich and protect us from all harm. Even Israel suffered quite a bit, even though they are His chosen people. But it does mean that He will carry us through the valleys as well as the mountain peaks. He will pour His blessings of faithfulness, hope, purpose, assurance of salvation, and more into the well of our lives.

Obadiah's prophecy shows us that God is the Almighty Restorer, not just in carrying out justice, but also by bestowing countless undeserved blessings upon us both here and in eternity.

***

I hope you enjoyed this journey through Obadiah as much as I did. Further, I pray you experienced first-hand how every book of the Bible (even the most obscure and unknown ones) can lend us fabulous insights into God and His truth. May He bless you tremendously as you seek to apply these rich truths to your life, and may He fuel your curiosity about Him through other books in His Word. Above all and through His Spirit, may He help you to be diligent to present yourself approved to Him as a workman who does not need to be ashamed, accurately handling His word of truth (2 Timothy 2:15).

BIBLIOGRAPHY

Baker, David W., T. Desmond Alexander, and Bruce K. Waltke. *Obadiah, Jonah, Micah: Tyndale Old Testament Commentaries.* Vol. 26. Downer's Grove: InterVarsity Press, 2009.

Baker, David W. *Joel, Obadiah, Malachi: The NIV Application Commentary.* Grand Rapids, MI: Zondervan, 2006. 161.

Carson, DA. "Exodus 5; Luke 8; Job 22; 1 Corinthians 9." For the Love of God Exodus 5 Luke 8 Job 22 1 Corinthians 9 Comments. February 22, 2015. Accessed February 24, 2015. http://www.thegospelcoalition.org/blogs/loveofgod/2015/02/22/exodus-5-luke-8-job-22-1-corinthians-9/.

"Depraved Indifference Law & Legal Definition." Depraved Indifference Law & Legal Definition. Accessed February 17, 2015. http://definitions.uslegal.com/d/depraved-indifference/.

Douglas, J., & Tenney, M. (Eds.). (1987). *Bible Dictionary.* Grand Rapids, MI: Zondervan.

Furby, Mindi Jo. *More than Words: Understanding the Ancient Book in a Modern World.* Bluffton, SC: MJF Publishing, 2013.

"Greek Lexicon :: G2491 (NASB)." Blue Letter Bible. Accessed 3 Feb, 2015.
http://www.blueletterbible.org/lang/lexicon/lexicon.cfm?Strongs=G2491&t=NASB

"Hebrew Lexicon :: H6 (NASB)." Blue Letter Bible. Accessed 12 Feb, 2015.
http://www.blueletterbible.org/lang/lexicon/lexicon.cfm?Strongs=H6&t=NASB

"Hebrew Lexicon :: H343 (NASB)." Blue Letter Bible. Accessed 18 Feb, 2015.
http://www.blueletterbible.org/lang/lexicon/lexicon.cfm?Strongs=H343&t=NASB

"Hebrew Lexicon :: H1368 (NASB)." Blue Letter Bible. Accessed 12 Feb, 2015.
http://www.blueletterbible.org/lang/lexicon/lexicon.cfm?Strongs=H1368&t=NASB

"Hebrew Lexicon :: H1431 (NASB)." Blue Letter Bible. Accessed 18 Feb, 2015.
http://www.blueletterbible.org/lang/lexicon/lexicon.cfm?Strongs=H1431&t=NASB

"Hebrew Lexicon :: H1471 (NASB)." Blue Letter Bible. Accessed 5 Feb, 2015.
http://www.blueletterbible.org/lang/lexicon/lexicon.cfm?Strongs=H1471&t=NASB

"Hebrew Lexicon :: H2009 (NASB)." Blue Letter Bible. Accessed 5 Feb, 2015.
http://www.blueletterbible.org/lang/lexicon/lexicon.cfm?Strongs=H2009&t=NASB

"Hebrew Lexicon :: H2377 (NASB)." Blue Letter Bible. Accessed 26 Jan, 2015.
http://www.blueletterbible.org/lang/lexicon/lexicon.cfm?Strongs=H2377&t=NASB

"Hebrew Lexicon :: H2865 (NASB)." Blue Letter Bible. Accessed 12 Feb, 2015.
http://www.blueletterbible.org/lang/lexicon/lexicon.cfm?Strongs=H2865&t=NASB

"Hebrew Lexicon :: H3680 (NASB)." Blue Letter Bible. Accessed 17 Feb, 2015.
http://www.blueletterbible.org/lang/lexicon/lexicon.cfm?Strongs=H3680&t=NASB

"Hebrew Lexicon :: H6413 (NASB)." Blue Letter Bible. Accessed 24 Feb, 2015.
http://www.blueletterbible.org/lang/lexicon/lexicon.cfm?Strongs=H6413&t=NASB

"Hebrew Lexicon :: H6869 (NASB)." Blue Letter Bible. Accessed 18 Feb, 2015.
http://www.blueletterbible.org/lang/lexicon/lexicon.cfm?Strongs=H6869&t=NASB

"Hebrew Lexicon :: H7451 (NASB)." Blue Letter Bible. Accessed 18 Feb, 2015. http://www.blueletterbible.org/lang/lexicon/lexicon.cfm?Strongs=H7451&t=NASB

"Hebrew Lexicon :: H8052 (NASB)." Blue Letter Bible. Accessed 5 Feb, 2015. http://www.blueletterbible.org/lang/lexicon/lexicon.cfm?Strongs=H8052&t=NASB

"Hebrew Lexicon :: H8055 (NASB)." Blue Letter Bible. Accessed 18 Feb, 2015. http://www.blueletterbible.org/lang/lexicon/lexicon.cfm?Strongs=H8055&t=NASB

"Hebrew Lexicon :: H955 (NASB)." Blue Letter Bible. Accessed 17 Feb, 2015. http://www.blueletterbible.org/lang/lexicon/lexicon.cfm?Strongs=H955&t=NASB

Lewis, C.S. *Mere Christianity*. New York: MacMillan Pub., 1952

"John - Boy | Ranked #45 on BabyCenter." BabyCenter. Accessed February 3, 2015. http://www.babycenter.com/baby-names-john-2330.htm.

Pfeiffer, Charles F. Baker's Bible Atlas. Grand Rapids, MI: Baker Book House, 2003.

Raabe, P. R. *Obadiah: A New Translation with Introduction and Commentary*. New York: Doubleday, 1996.

Sykes, Josephine, Monica Halpin, and Victor Brown. "Sir Winston Churchill: A Biography – Churchill College." Sir Winston Churchill: A Biography – Churchill College. Accessed July 01, 2016. https://www.chu.cam.ac.uk/archives/collections/churchill-papers/churchill-biography/

Walton, John H. *Zondervan Illustrated Bible Backgrounds Commentary*. Vol. 5. Grand Rapids, MI: Zondervan, 2009.

Young, Robert. *Analytical Concordance to the Bible*. Peabody, MA: Hendrickson Publishers, 1992.

ENDNOTES

[I] "Hebrew Lexicon :: H2377 (NASB)." Blue Letter Bible. Accessed 26 Jan, 2015. http://www.blueletterbible.org/lang/lexicon/lexicon.cfm?Strongs=H2377&t=NASB

[II] Douglas, J., & Tenney, M. (Eds.). (1987). *Bible Dictionary*. Grand Rapids, MI: Zondervan. p. 1052

[III] Douglas, *Bible Dictionary*, 1987, p. 1052

[IV] Douglas, *Bible Dictionary*, 1987, p. 1052

[V] Douglas, *Bible Dictionary*, 1987, p. 1052

[VI] Baker, David W., T. Desmond Alexander, and Bruce K. Waltke. *Obadiah, Jonah, Micah: Tyndale Old Testament Commentaries*. Vol. 26. Downer's Grove: InterVarsity Press, 2009, p. 31

[VII] Walton, John H. *Zondervan Illustrated Bible Backgrounds Commentary*. Vol. 5. Grand Rapids, MI: Zondervan, 2009, p. 93

[VIII] Baker, *Obadiah, Jonah, Micah: Tyndale Old Testament Commentaries*, 2009, p. 23

[IX] Baker, *Obadiah, Jonah, Micah: Tyndale Old Testament Commentaries*, 2009, p. 23

[X] "John - Boy | Ranked #45 on BabyCenter" This is incomplete

[XI] Baker, *Joel, Obadiah, Malachi: The NIV Application Commentary*, 2006, p. 146

[XII] Baker, *Joel, Obadiah, Malachi: The NIV Application Commentary*, 2006, p. 162

[XIII] Baker, *Joel, Obadiah, Malachi: The NIV Application Commentary*, 2006, p. 162

[XIV] Baker, *Obadiah, Jonah, Micah: Tyndale Old Testament Commentaries*, 2009, p. 31

[XV] Baker, *Joel, Obadiah, Malachi: The NIV Application Commentary*, 2006, p. 162

[XVI] Baker, *Joel, Obadiah, Malachi: The NIV Application Commentary*, 2006, p. 163

[XVII] Douglas, *Bible Dictionary*, 1987, p. 291

[XVIII] Douglas, *Bible Dictionary*, 1987, p. 292-293

[XIX] Douglas, *Bible Dictionary*, 1987, p. 292-293

[XX] Douglas, *Bible Dictionary*, 1987, p. 292-293

[XXI] Baker, *Obadiah, Jonah, Micah: Tyndale Old Testament Commentaries*, 2009, p. 32

[XXII] Refer to Week One for more details, but Obadiah was a common

Israelite name back then, meaning "Servant of the Lord."

XXIII "Hebrew Lexicon :: H8052 (NASB)." Blue Letter Bible. Accessed 5 Feb, 2015. http://www.blueletterbible.org/lang/lexicon/lexicon.cfm?Strongs=H8052&t=NASB

XXIV Walton, *Zondervan Illustrated Bible Backgrounds Commentary*, 2009, p. 94

XXV Walton, *Zondervan Illustrated Bible Backgrounds Commentary*, 2009, p. 94

XXVI Walton, *Zondervan Illustrated Bible Backgrounds Commentary*, 2009, p. 94

XXVII "Hebrew Lexicon :: H1471 (NASB)." Blue Letter Bible. Accessed 5 Feb, 2015. http://www.blueletterbible.org/lang/lexicon/lexicon.cfm?Strongs=H1471&t=NASB

XXVIII Baker, *Obadiah, Jonah, Micah: Tyndale Old Testament Commentaries*, 2009, p. 33

XXIX Baker, *Obadiah, Jonah, Micah: Tyndale Old Testament Commentaries*, 2009, p. 33

XXX Romans 8:28

XXXI "Hebrew Lexicon :: H2009 (NASB)." Blue Letter Bible. Accessed 5 Feb, 2015. http://www.blueletterbible.org/lang/lexicon/lexicon.cfm?Strongs=H2009&t=NASB

XXXII Walton, *Zondervan Illustrated Bible Backgrounds Commentary*, 2009,

p. 92

XXXIII Baker, *Joel, Obadiah, Malachi: The NIV Application Commentary*, 2006, p. 164

XXXIV Baker, *Joel, Obadiah, Malachi: The NIV Application Commentary*, 2006, p. 164

XXXV Baker, *Obadiah, Jonah, Micah: Tyndale Old Testament Commentaries*, 2009, p. 35

XXXVI Walton, *Zondervan Illustrated Bible Backgrounds Commentary*, 2009, p. 94

XXXVII Baker, *Joel, Obadiah, Malachi: The NIV Application Commentary*, 2006, p. 164

XXXVIII Walton, *Zondervan Illustrated Bible Backgrounds Commentary*, 2009, p. 94

XXXIX Douglas, *Bible Dictionary*, 1987, p. 160

XL Douglas, *Bible Dictionary*, 1987, p. 160

XLI http://www.baldeagleinfo.com/eagle/eagle4.html

XLII Lewis, *Mere Christianity*, 1952.

XLIII Baker, *Joel, Obadiah, Malachi: The NIV Application Commentary*, 2006, p. 170

XLIV Sykes, Josephine, Monica Halpin, and Victor Brown. "Sir Winston Churchill: A Biography – Churchill College." Sir Winston Churchill: A Biography – Churchill College. Accessed July 01, 2016. https://www.chu.cam.ac.uk/archives/collections/churchill-papers/churchill-biography/.

XLV Baker, *Joel, Obadiah, Malachi: The NIV Application Commentary*, 2006, p. 170

XLVI Douglas, *Bible Dictionary*, 1987, p. 238

XLVII Baker, *Obadiah, Jonah, Micah: Tyndale Old Testament Commentaries*, 2009, p. 37

XLVIII Baker, *Joel, Obadiah, Malachi: The NIV Application Commentary*, 2006, p. 171. By the way, scribal errors don't indicate theological discrepancies within the pages of Scripture. There are a few dozen textual variations within the numerous copies of Scripture's manuscripts, but none of them shed a questioning light on theology.

XLIX Baker, *Joel, Obadiah, Malachi: The NIV Application Commentary*, 2006, p. 171

L Baker, *Obadiah, Jonah, Micah: Tyndale Old Testament Commentaries*, 2009, p. 38

LI Baker, *Obadiah, Jonah, Micah: Tyndale Old Testament Commentaries*, 2009, p. 37

LII Baker, *Joel, Obadiah, Malachi: The NIV Application Commentary*, 2006, p. 175

LIII Baker, *Joel, Obadiah, Malachi: The NIV Application Commentary*, 2006, p. 175

LIV Baker, *Joel, Obadiah, Malachi: The NIV Application Commentary*, 2006, p. 175

LV "Hebrew Lexicon :: H6 (NASB)." Blue Letter Bible. Accessed 12 Feb,

2015.
http://www.blueletterbible.org/lang/lexicon/lexicon.cfm?Strongs=H6&t=NASB

LVI Baker, *Joel, Obadiah, Malachi: The NIV Application Commentary*, 2006, p. 175

LVII "Hebrew Lexicon :: H1368 (NASB)." Blue Letter Bible. Accessed 12 Feb, 2015.
http://www.blueletterbible.org/lang/lexicon/lexicon.cfm?Strongs=H1368&t=NASB

LVIII "Hebrew Lexicon :: H2865 (NASB)." Blue Letter Bible. Accessed 12 Feb, 2015.
http://www.blueletterbible.org/lang/lexicon/lexicon.cfm?Strongs=H2865&t=NASB

LIX Baker, *Joel, Obadiah, Malachi: The NIV Application Commentary*, 2006, p. 175-176

LX Baker, *Joel, Obadiah, Malachi: The NIV Application Commentary*, 2006, p. 151

LXI Raabe, P. R. *Obadiah: A New Translation with Introduction and Commentary*, 1996, p. 166

LXII Baker, *Obadiah, Jonah, Micah: Tyndale Old Testament Commentaries*, 2009, p. 39

LXIII Baker, *Joel, Obadiah, Malachi: The NIV Application Commentary*, 2006, p. 179

LXIV Special note: God is opposed to violence, but He does sanction bloodshed for punishment and in cases of justified war. The consequence of sin is death—the shedding of blood—which Christ paid on our behalf. Sometimes (as in Edom's case), God sheds blood to stop violence. God is a warrior Himself—the only true and righteous One. For more information on this topic, read *God is a Warrior* by Tremper Longman III and Daniel G. Reid.

LXV http://www.bjs.gov/content/pub/pdf/ipv9310.pdf

LXVI "Hebrew Lexicon :: H3680 (NASB)." Blue Letter Bible. Accessed 17 Feb, 2015. http://www.blueletterbible.org/lang/lexicon/lexicon.cfm?Strongs=H3680&t=NASB

LXVII "Hebrew Lexicon :: H955 (NASB)." Blue Letter Bible. Accessed 17 Feb, 2015. http://www.blueletterbible.org/lang/lexicon/lexicon.cfm?Strongs=H955&t=NASB

LXVIII Baker, *Joel, Obadiah, Malachi: The NIV Application Commentary*, 2006, p. 180

LXIX Baker, *Joel, Obadiah, Malachi: The NIV Application Commentary*, 2006, p. 180

LXX Baker, *Joel, Obadiah, Malachi: The NIV Application Commentary*, 2006, p. 180

LXXI http://definitions.uslegal.com/d/depraved-indifference/

LXXII Douglas, *Bible Dictionary*, 1987, p. 601

LXXIII Baker, *Joel, Obadiah, Malachi:* the NIV Application Commentary, 2006, p. 180

LXXIV The following translations take liberty in translating this and the next verses as past tense instead of present: King James Version, New

King James Version, New Living Translation, Revised Standard Version, Darby Translation, and Webster's Translation. Those translating it correctly in the present tense include the New American Standard Bible, the New International Version, the English Standard Version, and the Holman Christian Standard Bible.

LXXV Baker, *Joel, Obadiah, Malachi: The NIV Application Commentary*, 2006, p. 181

LXXVI Baker, *Joel, Obadiah, Malachi: The NIV Application Commentary*, 2006, p. 181

LXXVII "Hebrew Lexicon :: H8055 (NASB)." Blue Letter Bible. Accessed 18 Feb, 2015.
http://www.blueletterbible.org/lang/lexicon/lexicon.cfm?Strongs=H8055&t=NASB

LXXVIII "Hebrew Lexicon :: H6 (NASB)." Blue Letter Bible. Accessed 18 Feb, 2015.
http://www.blueletterbible.org/lang/lexicon/lexicon.cfm?Strongs=H6&t=NASB

LXXIX "Hebrew Lexicon :: H1431 (NASB)." Blue Letter Bible. Accessed 18 Feb, 2015.
http://www.blueletterbible.org/lang/lexicon/lexicon.cfm?Strongs=H1431&t=NASB

LXXX It's also used this way in Ezekiel 35:13, Joel 2:20, Lamentations 1:9, Zephaniah 2:8, Psalm 35:26 and 38:17.

LXXXI "Hebrew Lexicon :: H6869 (NASB)." Blue Letter Bible. Accessed 18 Feb, 2015.
http://www.blueletterbible.org/lang/lexicon/lexicon.cfm?Strongs=H6869&t=NASB

LXXXII Carson, "Exodus 5; Luke 8; Job 22; 1 Corinthians 9"

LXXXIII "Hebrew Lexicon :: H343 (NASB)." Blue Letter Bible. Accessed 18 Feb, 2015.
http://www.blueletterbible.org/lang/lexicon/lexicon.cfm?Strongs=H343&t=NASB

LXXXIV "Hebrew Lexicon :: H7451 (NASB)." Blue Letter Bible. Accessed 18 Feb, 2015.
http://www.blueletterbible.org/lang/lexicon/lexicon.cfm?Strongs=H7451&t=NASB

LXXXV Some commentators believe exile, not death, is what's being communicated here, since "survivors" are mentioned in the next part of the verse. I respectfully disagree, however, because of the Hebrew word used and its previous context within Obadiah. While not all fugitives would have been "cut down" and killed (the context doesn't suggest comprehensiveness either), some undoubtedly would have. It was a military attack, after all, and Israel's history shows they were not unfamiliar with being victims of violence.

LXXXVI Baker, *Obadiah, Jonah, Micah: Tyndale Old Testament Commentaries*, 2009, p. 42

LXXXVII Douglas, *Bible Dictionary*, 1987, p. 322

LXXXVIII Baker, *Joel, Obadiah, Malachi: The NIV Application Commentary*, 2006, p. 190

LXXXIX Baker, *Joel, Obadiah, Malachi: The NIV Application Commentary*, 2006, p. 190

XC Baker, *Joel, Obadiah, Malachi: The NIV Application Commentary*, 2006, p. 190

XCI Psalm 3:4, 48:1; Isaiah 56:7, 57:13, 65:11; Ezekiel 20:40, 28:14; Daniel 9:16, 20; Joel 2:1, 3:17; Zechariah 8:3; 2 Peter 1:18.

XCII "Hebrew Lexicon :: H6413 (NASB)." Blue Letter Bible. Accessed 24 Feb, 2015. http://www.blueletterbible.org/lang/lexicon/lexicon.cfm?Strongs=H6413&t=NASB

XCIII Baker, *Obadiah, Jonah, Micah: Tyndale Old Testament Commentaries*, 2009, p. 44

XCIV Baker, *Joel, Obadiah, Malachi: The NIV Application Commentary*, 2006, p. 191

XCV Baker, *Obadiah, Jonah, Micah: Tyndale Old Testament Commentaries*, 2009, p. 44

XCVI Several examples of purging sin through punishment are found throughout Scripture, including Deuteronomy 13:5, 17:7, 19:19, 22:22; Exodus 20:38; and Daniel 11:35.

XCVII An interesting note: the phrase "house of Esau" occurs nowhere else in the Bible. It was "minted by Obadiah to provide a formal counterpart to the other two houses in the verse and as a play on the fraternal relationship between Esau and Jacob." Baker, Joel, Obadiah, Malachi: *The NIV Application Commentary*, 2006, p. 192

XCVIII Baker, *Joel, Obadiah, Malachi: The NIV Application Commentary*, 2006, p. 192

XCIX Acts of total destruction include the flood (Genesis 6) and when the Israelites began their military campaign against those who formerly occupied the Promised Land (Joshua 9:24).

C Baker, *Obadiah, Jonah, Micah: Tyndale Old Testament Commentaries*, 2009, p. 45

CI Consider the creation account as one of the most powerful displays of God's words. He literally spoke the universe into existence and declared that everything was "good." If He can do that with simple words, carrying out a prophecy against a tiny nation like Edom is not much of a challenge.

CII Pfeiffer, *Baker's Bible Atlas*, 2003, p. 321

CIII Baker, *Joel, Obadiah, Malachi: The NIV Application Commentary*, 2006, p. 196

CIV Baker, *Joel, Obadiah, Malachi: The NIV Application Commentary*, 2006, p. 197

CV Baker, *Joel, Obadiah, Malachi: The NIV Application Commentary*, 2006, p. 197

CVI Baker, *Joel, Obadiah, Malachi: The NIV Application Commentary*, 2006, p. 198

CVII Baker, *Joel, Obadiah, Malachi: The NIV Application Commentary*, 2006, p. 198

CVIII For a more in-depth analysis of canonical history, please read *More than Words* by Mindi Jo Furby

CIX Baker, *Obadiah, Jonah, Micah: Tyndale Old Testament Commentaries*, 2009, p. 47

CX Baker, *Obadiah, Jonah, Micah: Tyndale Old Testament Commentaries*, 2009, p. 47

CXI Baker, *Joel, Obadiah, Malachi: The NIV Application Commentary*, 2006, p. 199-200

CXII Douglas, *Bible Dictionary*, 1987, p. 188

CXIII Baker, *Joel, Obadiah, Malachi: The NIV Application Commentary*, 2006, p. 199

CXIV Baker, *Joel, Obadiah, Malachi: The NIV Application Commentary*, 2006, p. 199

CXV Young, *Analytical Concordance to the Bible*, 1992. P. 838-39

CXVI Baker, *Joel, Obadiah, Malachi: The NIV Application Commentary*, 2006, p. 198

CXVII Baker, *Obadiah, Jonah, Micah: Tyndale Old Testament Commentaries*, 2009, p. 48